THE
CARING
CONGREGATION

THE CARING CONGREGATION

How to become one and why it matters

Karen Lampe

Abingdon Press
Nashville

THE CARING CONGREGATION
HOW TO BECOME ONE AND
WHY IT MATTERS

This book is printed on acid-free paper.

Library of Congress Cataloging-in-Publication Data

Lampe, Karen.
The caring congregation : how to become one and why it matters / Karen Lampe.
    p. cm.
Includes bibliographical references.
ISBN 978-1-4267-2733-7 (trade pbk. : alk. paper) 1. Church work with the sick. 2. Church work with the bereaved. 3. Caring—Religious aspects—Christianity. I. Title.
BV4460.L36 2011
259—dc22

2011011979

11 12 13 14 15 16 17 18 19 20—10 9 8 7 6 5 4 3 2 1

MANUFACTURED IN THE UNITED STATES OF AMERICA

Lovingly dedicated to the congregation of

The United Methodist Church of the Resurrection,

which has allowed me to learn through its journeys

Contents

Introduction

So deeply do we care for you that we are determined to
share with you not only the gospel of God but also our
own selves, because you have become very dear to us.
—1 *Thessalonians* 2:8

L ife is messy and often painful. No one can avoid the grief and loss that happens in all of our lives at some point. What we do to help one another get through difficult times can be complex, yet it can be so simple. As people of faith committed to healing and wholeness, sometimes we can just show up and reach out. Other times, we offer words of comfort or a listening ear.

Our ministry of Congregational Care (CC) at The United Methodist Church of the Resurrection is carefully designed to connect with people during their difficult times. It started with our founding pastor, Adam Hamilton. He, like all of us, takes the responsibility for the care of our members very seriously. Our CC ministry has steadily evolved since the church's beginning in 1990, yet what we have today is a ministry, like our members, that is on the way to perfection. Through our congregational care, we continually strive to create new ways in which compassionate ministry can happen. We believe this ministry is vital to our goals and mission.

In our church, caregiving initially consisted of Adam and a few volunteers; then an associate pastor and seminary students began helping; and now, we have an entire department dedicated to the task. We believe one reason our church has grown is because hurting people find not only relief but also hope and companionship. Currently our CC team includes seven full-time pastors, an executive director who is also a pastor, two seminary interns, and a retired pastor. We also have a full-time funeral and wedding director, four full-time administrative assistants, a baptism administrator, a full-time family counselor who supervises our mental health interns, and a host of unpaid staff whom we call our Congregational Care Ministers (CCMs). This group of volunteers is key to how we do ministry. We train and empower them to take on the tasks of care that they might not have otherwise seen themselves capable of doing. It is a joy and a blessing to watch them grow as they practice their faith.

However, for most faith communities, a large staff is not an option, so being creative and inviting others into the ministry of care is important. This book will help you devise a plan for your congregational care. If you are considering being a caregiver, this book is also meant to help you grasp basic principles and skills. But whatever brings you to this book, as you read it, keep asking yourself these four questions:

WHAT is God calling me to do?

WHAT are my priorities and goals?

WHO can help me?

WHAT are the ways I can accomplish each goal?

The Purpose of This Book

Jesus was a healer. You only need to read the Gospel of Luke to find the multiple times that Jesus healed bodies, minds, and spirits. He understood the depths of suffering and its stranglehold on the lives of people. He did not learn this from formal training but rather from his intimate connection to God, and this allowed him to extend understanding and empathy. As caregivers, this is our task too, and the purpose of this book is to try to give words and clues so that you may offer Christlike healing.

First and foremost, anyone embarking on the task of being a Christian caregiver must always seek ways to be transformed into a Christlike healer. Sometimes this means taking stock of your own life lessons, those experiences that help us become wounded healers. And, as it did with Jesus and the woman who was about to be stoned by her accusers, it may mean getting your hands dirty. Jesus got down in the dirt, literally and figuratively, with the woman. He wrote in the dirt. He showed kindness to a woman whose crime was considered "dirty." His purpose was more than to save the woman's life and bring insight to her accusers; it was to bring healing and wholeness, thereby preparing all of them to receive God's redemptive gift of grace. In these actions he was bold, but he was also careful.

Anyone who is a healer seeks the ability to be bold yet grace-filled. You can tell those caregivers who "get it" by what they say and do. They cannot help themselves; they are drawn to the depressed, the downtrodden, the marginalized, the grieving, or the dying. I have worked with people who "get it" intuitively as well as those who are more task-oriented. In ministry we need both kinds of people, and both kinds benefit from the gifts and graces of the other. This book will help prepare you with the how-to for getting down in the dirt with people in order to offer healing and compassion.

Finally, healing ministry is about the collective body and all of its constitutive parts. As a healer, you have to understand your particular context and how it affects your community. If there is a financial crisis going on, you have to be keenly aware of what is necessary and possible. If there have been a multitude of deaths, you still have to be able to find ways for healing to happen. If there is deep segregation, disparity of roles, or injustice, you have to be willing to address what is necessary for the larger community.

No one person, lay or clergy, can address all the hurt of a congregation or community. Caregiving is not a job for Lone Rangers. Your job as a leader is to evaluate the needs of your community and then prioritize them as you assess available resources. As your ministry blossoms, you can begin to invite others to help you create a comprehensive healing ministry through a variety of means: teaching, worship, study, counseling, support groups, and so on.

How to Use This Book

There are four chapters in this book. They are designed to give you the basics to offer systematic congregational care: prayer ministry, support ministry, hospital visitation, and grief and death ministry. In my ministry, I've found that these are foundational for most churches.

At the beginning of each chapter, there is a case study. These are meant to be examples and are written in my words and based on actual events. However, to protect confidentiality, the names of the people and places involved have been changed to protect their identities. Further, we also obtained their permission for the use of their stories. These are all stories of redemption. I hope that you will read them carefully and put yourself in the story as not only the caregiver but also the person receiving care.

Redemption is key to caregiving. The simple definition of *redemption* is to restore. Restore to what? Restored to being the whole person God intends you to be, a person who lives a grace-filled life in service to God and other people, a person who communes with God and whose character is marked by the fruits of the Spirit as found in Galatians 5:22-23. Good congregational care offers redemption—restoration—as we partner with God to care for weary, heavy-laden souls and those souls who are just trying to hang on and cope. Redemption can mean healing of relationships or restoration of a community.

Through our acts of care, people can find restoration in the middle of death and grief, and they can find it in our simple acts of kindness. When we think about congregational care in this way, it becomes both the cornerstone and aim for everything else we do in ministry.

After the redemption story—case study—is told, we will explore methods, practical skills, and tools that will help you in your setting. My hope is that you will be inspired as well as equipped.

The ministry of congregational care takes patience and a non-judgmental approach. It can be complex, exhausting, and perplexing (sometimes all at once), and you need a confidant for your own well-being. You'll need to debrief and sometimes laugh and cry with a trusted someone, even as you continue to honor confidentiality. Just a quick word of advice: don't use your spouse or family. Seek someone else; a professional caregiver or counselor is best. Caregiving is like almost everything else, the more you do it, the more you'll realize how little you actually know and how much help you really need.

Healing can be fast, or it may be very, very slow. And on this side of heaven, none of us is ever entirely whole. While different facets of a healing ministry can be taught through volumes and volumes of texts, it is best learned through practice and then being open to the suggestions of peers, mentors, and even sometimes those for whom we care.

As you create your own care team or become more involved in the congregational care of your church, keep in mind that there is a need to collaborate with every part of the church. *Let the entire church embrace this ministry* so that they too can see its benefits. Help the church see that congregational care is their ministry too. It is a ministry of all the people, not just a specialized group.

My prayer for you is that by using this book, you will be able to take your congregational care to the next level in your own ministry setting as you offer redemption to those in need.

CHAPTER ONE

In All Things: PRAY FIRST!

Devote yourselves to prayer, being watchful and thankful.
—Colossians 4:2 NIV

All of us in ministry understand that prayer should always be our starting place for everything, but sometimes we take the power of prayer for granted.

Your journey of creating a congregational care ministry or directing people in their journey to help you should start with prayer.

So, to begin, may I pray for you?

> *Prayer: O healing God, we give you thanks for the opportunity to serve your people. We give you thanks for being appointed to do this holy task. Yet we don't know and are unsure of how to prioritize needs and create the systems that will best meet their needs. So Lord, I pray for anyone who is starting this journey. Give them courage and strength to know that you will guide them. Please provide them with vision, understanding, and resources. Help them not to be afraid to ask for help. And in all of this, we will give you the praise as we point your people to your healing grace and love.*
>
> *In Christ's name. Amen.*

The Redemptive Force of Prayer

As you recall from the Introduction, in each chapter a redemptive story or stories will be used to illustrate the ministry that happens through Congregational Care. *Redemption means the act of restoring.* The importance of prayer for redemption in all situations is primary. Let me illustrate through a personal story.

Easter Sunday had finally arrived. That morning promised to be one of the best Easter Sundays ever for The Church of the Resurrection. The weather was exceptional, spring break was over, and the sports schedule was minimal. However, the week before had been brutal in other ways as our department tended to the needs of eight families in the congregation who had experienced a death. For three of those funerals, I had been the lead pastor to attend to the services and the families. So when the sun came up that morning, although I felt charged with energy for the day, I have to say I was running on near empty.

I arrived at the church before our earliest service at 7 a.m., parked along the far edges of the parking lot, and began to walk into church. My arms were laden with my robe, stole, two clean shirts, two pairs of shoes, and two bags of other needed items. As I began to walk briskly (nearly breaking into a jog), I felt myself begin to stumble. As I continued at my quick pace, I completely lost my balance, then went face first toward the pavement. As the left side of my face ate gravel and I felt my glasses give way, I thought, *This is not good.*

Lying there for just a very brief moment, I hoped that someone had seen the fall, yet also in my embarrassment, I was hoping no one had seen me plummet. Well, it proved to be the latter, so I picked myself up and quickly realized I was bleeding from my mouth, nose, and the scrapes up to my left eye.

As it turned out, I was taken by ambulance to the nearest hospital. But the prayers that occurred in between the time the accident happened until I got home around one o'clock tell something about prayer and the restoration that happens through the redemptive process.

Again, I was reminded of my primary contention about prayer: **Prayer lifts us up out of the chaos of the moment to a different reality. That reality is where we connect with God and where restoration can happen.**

With that in mind, I'll try to relay to you very briefly the number of prayers that either someone said for me, or I said for someone else on that Easter morning:

1. The medical doctor who volunteers his care for our congregation during worship services prayed for me and I prayed for him.

2. Our pastors came and prayed over me individually before I was shipped to the hospital.

3. On the way to the hospital I prayed for the young EMT in the ambulance who told me she and her partner could not find a welcoming church.

4. I prayed with the custodian in the ER who said he was working three jobs and wouldn't make it to church on Easter Sunday.

5. My husband and I prayed with the young man who shared our large room in the ER. He shouted that he was scared and asked us to open the curtain separating us.

Whenever someone was praying for me or I was praying for someone else, we were in the act of restoring. We were transcending the chaos of the moment. We were connecting with God.

That crazy Easter morning that I'll never forget was full of opportunities for people to be touched by God's love—including me! After that morning, I received many calls, cards, Facebook messages, and e-mails from people telling me they were praying for me. And I truly believe those prayers accounted for why I healed so quickly.

Principles of Prayer at Resurrection

Every church and pastor has basic ideas about how to do their daily ministry. For me, prayer absolutely sets the tone and flow for the day. My hope is that this extends out into the congregation in amazing ways. *Prayer is the means by which people expect the pastor to connect with God*, yet so many times I think pastors are reticent to say, "I'd like to pray for you. Would that be OK?"

Let me explain to you some key ways that prayer is extended at our church.

First of all, the pastors, directors, and leaders understand that every meeting, class, or service begins and ends with prayer. That prayer usually includes thanksgiving to God, a request for God's guiding presence, and acknowledgment of any obvious needs of those assembled.

Pastoral Prayer: in our worship services we try to use clear language that uses all the parts of prayer as described in the acronym ACTS.

A-Adoration

C-Confession

T-Thanksgiving

S-Supplication

We assume there are people who may not have been in church for a long time, so we create prayers that speak to the possible needs of the individual, congregation, or country. We do not preach through our prayers, but rather we try to take people out of the chaos of the world, and help them rise above whatever is hurting or worrying them. This is a very pastoral time. We want to lead people to a holy place so they can truly worship. Once they are centered, they can receive the Scriptures and sermon for the day. Never underestimate the power of a great pastoral prayer.

Prayer requests for the bulletin are so important to the congregation. Whether someone has a new baby, is facing a life-threatening illness, or is sending a loved one off to war, people want to enlist their community of faith to pray with them. Yet, depending on the size of your congregation, you want to approach this carefully.

Over the years we have decreased the space for our prayer requests in the weekly bulletin. We have done this partly because we have felt a need to be very careful about which joys and concerns we make public, but also because we have developed other ways for people to receive or to be in prayer.

One of our most important means of enlisting prayer has been through our **Covenant Prayer Team.** This team receives lists of prayer requests throughout the week. Just today I received a list of three people who called or e-mailed asking for care or prayer. Sometimes the list is ten people. Only the first name is given to this team of people and a general description of what is requested by those asking for prayer. In this manner, we can keep daily prayers flowing through the life of the congregation.

Prayer Request Cards are provided in the seat backs in the sanctuary. People are encouraged to write down their requests during the service and then drop them in the offering plates after the service. People who worship online are also invited to submit their requests. This has worked very well for years, and most regular attendees know of this method of communication. However, it is very important occasionally to remind people of this opportunity to request prayer.

Every Sunday after the last service or very early Monday morning, one of our key staff members and a few volunteers sift through the multitude of prayer request cards for any emergencies that need our immediate attention. There may be a Monday morning surgery or someone in a crisis who cries out through a prayer card.

The cards are quickly copied and given to the pastors as they come in on Monday morning. The pastors and their teams look through them *prayerfully* and quickly access how to address the needs. Beyond that, the prayer cards are sent to a special prayer team who write prayer notes to each person regarding their request.

The best way I can tell you of how God works through this prayer is through an illustration that helped me learn years ago how important our prayers are. I received a card from a young woman who had written that her grandfather had passed away recently. I put the card into the usual pile for sympathy and grief, knowing that it would be addressed. But "something" kept bringing to my mind the young woman who had written the card, and by that afternoon I could not stand it any longer, and responded to the nudge.

The call began with the usual "Hi, how are you? This is Pastor Karen calling." But before I could get to the usual part about extending "my sympathy regarding the death of your grandfather," the young woman's voice broke and she said, "How did you know to call?" She went on to say she had just returned from the doctor who had told her that she had cancer.

This call hit me like a ton of bricks. What I came to understand was that God had been responding to me as I had been praying over the cards.

Before every counseling session, our pastors are encouraged to pray. This prayer of preparation allows you to care for yourself spiritually, emotionally, and mentally as you understand the rigors of such a session. Do not neglect to give yourself this gift!

As the counseling session begins, I always tell the party that I believe God is present and acts through grace to help us figure out what is happening in their particular situation. I want them to know this is a safe place. I tell them I'd like to start with prayer. The prayer usually goes something like this:

> *Gracious God, we thank you for the opportunity for John to share what is on his heart today. Allow him to dig deep and for me to listen with grace. Allow us to listen together to what you might be adding to this conversation. All this we pray in your Son's healing name. Amen.*

Many times after the short prayer the person is tearful and is more ready to open up for possible healing.

Perhaps more important is the prayer that the person receives at the end of the session. I truly believe that for most people, this moment of prayer is why they came for counseling. As you have listened carefully to their needs, fears, and questions throughout the session, allow God to speak through you.

Hospital visitation should be bathed in prayer. The chapter on hospital visitation contains practical tips to prepare you or your volunteers for this important ministry. Before you enter the room, say a silent prayer that God will use you to be a presence of calm and assurance.

Patients are in a very vulnerable situation and to have someone pray for them before surgery or during the healing process helps them transcend a situation in which they can feel powerless. I always ask patients what they want me to pray for before surgery. Often they have specific things going through their mind. Right before I pray I address those concerns. Two great Scriptures that address the fear or anxiety often felt before surgery are Isaiah 43:1-5a (do not fear) and 1 Peter 5:7-11 (cast all your anxiety on God).

After the Scriptures are read, I ask if I can anoint them with oil before prayer (James 5:14), and then I pray something like this:

> *Healing God, thank you so much that we can live in a day and an age of modern miracles. We thank you for this hospital and the wonderful nurses and doctors who are here to be the hands of Christ in their ministry. Lord, today I pray for that healing to come to _____ that she or he may receive the best care from all of her or his health-care providers. Allow them to offer the best of medicine and the kindest support. And even beyond this, God, we would ask that you who know every fiber of _____'s being, would bring complete healing. So Lord, prepare _____'s body so that he or she might receive complete healing this day. We also pray for _____'s family that*

you will strengthen them for the ministry of family. Help all present here today breathe deeply that they might release any fear or anxiety in this moment. We know you are here with us and that you will be present every moment. All this in Christ's name. Amen.

Prayer vigils are a wonderful way to draw people together to pray. We have two major prayer vigils each year, one on Thanksgiving and one on Good Friday. For each event we choose a special theme. We provide short, simple prayer guides for both children and adults. Small groups, Sunday school classes, or families are encouraged to attend together. Our prayer vigils usually start early in the morning, incorporate a short noontime program, and end with a meaningful closing service. Our congregation responds positively to these events, and they add a beautiful layer of meaning to those seasons.

Create holy spaces that encourage prayer. This past year our worship planning team took a field trip to various Catholic churches in our area. Most of them had strategic places set aside for prayer. They were usually set in a quiet area that allowed people to come and go without being noticed. At Resurrection, our Firestone Prayer Chapel is set outside the main sanctuary and is available daily for prayer. We are currently working on a Prayer Wall and a Prayer Walk that will be outdoor features. I am convinced that such holy spaces allow and encourage people to pray.

As you consider what sacred areas you might create for prayer, I would encourage you to supply a quiet space with writing materials, prayer guides, candles, Bibles, and chairs. You might also provide reading materials that offer guidance regarding life issues such as grief, miscarriage, divorce, unemployment, and the like.

We train our volunteers to pray out loud. Many times people are reluctant to pray out loud. Congregational Care volunteers must be able to pray with people on the phone, through an e-mail or other written correspondence, or in person. As leaders, we have a duty to teach people how to pray. We do not assume they will know how to do this. In the next section, I have outlined what we teach to congregants, volunteers, and staff about praying out loud.

Praying Out Loud

For the last several years we have offered Praying Out Loud classes for our congregants, key volunteers, and staff members. One of those resources is a book by Laurence Hull Stookey called *Let the Whole Church Say Amen! A Guide for Those Who Pray in Public*. The main goal of the class is to give people tools to be more comfortable when praying out loud for groups or when praying one-on-one.

Seven basic steps to this course include:

1. Teach the person always to ask God to give them a right heart and words before they begin to say anything.

2. Begin by studying the different prayer types in the Psalms.

3. Write prayers that praise God.

4. Learn to name God according to the situation (Healing God, Gracious God, and so forth).

5. Help people with their confessions so they can release their guilt and shame.

6. Make your petitions appropriate for the situation (forgiveness, comfort, strength).

7. Practice praying out loud when you are alone or with those with whom you are comfortable.

As a ministry leader, you will be an example to those around you. Be an encouraging leader! As you train others to pray, encourage them so that their confidence to pray will grow. Then they will follow your lead by encouraging others to pray.

Our Praying Out Loud class is the basic curriculum on prayer, but we have developed others as we have seen needs arise in our congregation. For instance, after a sermon series on marriage, we developed a study called Praying as a Couple.

BACK TO REDEMPTION . . .

Let's go back to my initial story that started with my fall on Easter. There are the obvious ways that the restoring forces of redemption were at play. There were people along my path that day whom I was able to pray with who were certainly out of the ordinary. Perhaps their lives would not have been touched by the Easter story if the accident had not happened.

There was a need for healing of my body. No doubt, rest was also a primary need. The prayers that were directed toward me that day and in the days ahead had a huge impact on my physical and emotional recovery.

All of this is pretty clear.

But the deeper redemptive process happened in my soul during those eight weeks of sabbatical. You know ministry is intense and draining. But in stepping away, I wrestled with the reasons for why I do ministry. I prayed daily that my zeal for serving God and others would be restored to greater heights than ever before. I prayed that I would have greater compassion and understanding for the staff and volunteers with whom I serve God.

Through these intense prayers I think I came back to some primary conclusions:

God is always speaking. If you keep getting a message, do not ignore it! One of our pastors recently told me that as she prepared for a funeral, she knew that the woman was a quilter, but it kept coming to her that she should talk about weaving at the funeral rather than quilting. She kept fighting the urge, until finally she gave in to the voice. What she did not know was that the daughter of the deceased was a weaver. For the daughter, the images of a weaver spoke beautifully about her mother's life.

WHO KNEW? God. And God kept trying to speak to the pastor. If we are only willing to listen, we will hear God speaking to us.

All this to say that as you are preparing yourself to prioritize the needs of your congregation and create a congregational care ministry, take some time to wrestle with God. God is speaking to you! What we might think as necessary for our congregation may be merely our own misdirected motives.

Take time for prayer daily! It may seem strange to say this to pastors and ministry leaders, but unless we are lifted up out of the chaos of the moment to a place where God can speak to us, we may never get the message. Unless, of course, you happen to be stopped in your tracks by a fall on Easter morning!

Hey, redemption happens.

Questions and Reflections

What is your daily prayer routine?

Do you allow time for a breath prayer for yourself between ministry appointments?

What does it mean for you to "Pray without ceasing"? How could you increase the number of times you pray each day?

What are routine activities that might give you daily prompts for prayer?

Some suggestions:

    getting in and out of the car

    entering or leaving a room

    hitting the "send" button on e-mail

    hanging up the phone

Enlist a colleague or a trusted congregant to discuss the following:

    What is your content and prayer strategy for worship?

    What is working?

    Why do you think it works?

    What needs to be improved?

Name some steps for designing a strategy for follow-up on prayer requests.

Do you currently:

    Have a formal procedure to collect prayer requests?

    Supply prayer cards in the pews?

    Have a method to process prayer requests?

Do you have a prayer team that regularly follows up with prayer requests?

If not, how could you develop one?

How could your ministry setting benefit from an increased focus on prayer?

What is the best forum in which to introduce this to your congregation?

A sermon series?

A short-term class on a specific aspect or style of prayer?

A prayer vigil or prayer walk centered around a holy day or specific event?

Name a time when you have seen redemption happen through a personal illness or injury. How did prayer transform the experience?

Suggested Resources on Prayer

Let the Whole Church Say Amen! A Guide for Those Who Pray in Public by Laurence Hull Stookey. Nashville: Abingdon Press, June 2001.

CHAPTER TWO

Support Ministries: Creating the Toolbox for Care

So deeply do we care for you that we are determined to
share with you not only the gospel of God but also our
own selves, because you have become very dear to us.
— *1 Thessalonians 2:8*

Stories of redemption where people, families, and whole communities are restored, or even completely transformed, are numerous in the ministry of Congregational Care. There have been days when I have thought I have heard it all, but then a new situation comes along and I'm learning all over again about the complexity of our lives and how God works in ways that are mysterious and wonderful.

With that in mind, let me begin with three short stories that will give you an idea of what I mean.

Redemption Story 1

The young woman came into my office with an obvious pained expression. She shyly shook my hand and sat down on the far side of the sofa. As we began our session I went through my regular explanations about God's grace. She started to tear up but offered only silence when I asked if she had any questions before she began to tell her story. I offered a brief prayer, then asked her to share what was on her heart.

She began by telling me that she had been an intern last summer with an area company. It was during that internship that a trusted male supervisor began to take special interest in her. One night when they were alone, he assaulted her. Confused, ashamed, and not knowing what to do, she kept the incident to herself. But the scenario repeated itself with new drama time after time. When she finally found herself pregnant, she told her parents.

The story became more and more complex as she had not filed for any child support and had very little conversation with the man after he learned she was pregnant. Apparently he had urged her to get an abortion, but she refused. At the time she came to me, the baby had already been born and she did not know how to move forward with her life.

Redemption Story 2

The distraught call came early in the morning. The voice on the other end was a young woman whose husband had confessed to her about having had multiple affairs. It seems that when he traveled for his business, he picked up women. Could she and her husband come in? They needed help immediately.

When they arrived, it was obvious that they shouldn't have been sitting in a public waiting room as both of them were crying intermittently. So I quickly called them back to my office and we began the process of unpacking the situation.

The young husband's job had kept him on the road during the week for many years. At first he had just visited Internet porn sites, but later found himself "hooking up" with women in the different cities. He could recount eighteen different partners.

After he relayed his story, I said to his wife: "Do you want to save this marriage?" She looked at her husband with an angry, confused, yet loving look. "Yes, I think I do. It's just so hard to comprehend this information."

I asked him the same question and he responded, "Oh, yes, but will she be able to forgive me? I cannot stand myself right now." Huge sobs.

We sat for just a minute. Like Job picking at his scabs, we just sat there in the mess of it all for a while.

And then I began to talk about the road of redemption with them that went something like this:

"For both of you this is going to be a long, difficult journey, but it can also be the most sanctifying ride of your life. Both of you need a savior right now. John, you need one, because the idea of forgiveness seems like a mountain you've got to climb and you can't see how you're going to do it. Cheryl, you need one, because today seems pretty dark, but you know there is a glimmer of light and that is what has brought you to your church.

"You've both heard the word *redemption* before, but now you're really going to have to own it. *Redemption* means restoring, but to be restored back to where trust was pure and untainted may not be possible. But what you can know is that you can be restored back to a better, wiser, stronger place where you understand the slippery slope of evil, a place where you understand the importance of your vows, a place where you understand the importance of rules, but you also believe in the power of grace. It is possible, but we've got to begin to set up a strategy. Let's talk about getting you into counseling, some marriage retreats, and decide who you can trust to be your confidants to help you individually and as a couple.

"Cheryl, do you understand that you will be able to help John be sanctified throughout this process by setting rules and standards, yet also by being grace-filled? John, do you understand that you will need to regain Cheryl's trust and that this will mean checking in more and allowing her to set the rules?

"Are we ready to start this journey?"

Resolutely, they both nodded as they looked at each other.

As the session ended, I suggested we go into the chapel to kneel and pray together. When we entered the quiet sacred spaces, I asked if they would join me at the altar. I asked them about their wedding vows and talked about "for better or worse." Then I opened my Bible to Psalm 51, which is a beautiful psalm attributed to David after his relations with Bathsheba. I read the part about: "Create in me a clean heart, O God, / and put a new and right spirit within me." John sobbed as he knelt at the altar.

Then I anointed them both with oil, asking for God's healing and restoration of their marriage.

This was the first of many opportunities to care for them in the years ahead. They have taken classes on praying together, gone on retreats, listened intently during forgiveness classes; and as they have healed, they have reached out to care for others going through similar situations.

Oh, sweet redemption!

Redemption Story 3

The first time Cindy introduced herself to me at church, I thought she had a wonderful sparkle. Her mom and dad were dear senior members, always sitting in the same spot. But Cindy seemed to be a loner at church, occasionally bringing a friend with her.

The night I received the first pager call from Cindy was very scary for me. I think it might have been my first call from a person threatening suicide.

Cindy started coming in for occasional sessions with me where we talked and prayed about her depression and alcoholism. She was trying to be faithful to AA and she went to an intensive rehab for a month that summer. By fall she was in a risky relationship and having trouble staying sober. This, of course, made her more depressed.

Then finally one night, with another suicide attempt, she succeeded.

I could not believe it. Her parents were devastated.

It felt as if we had failed.

Where was the redemption? Who was restored in this, God?

* * * * *

Out of each of these three stories, there is much to ponder and learn. Over the years, I have learned so much about how to navigate certain situations, but it never ceases to amaze me how God continues to teach me. With each person you encounter, there is so much opportunity for support ministry to happen in different ways.

Let's now move to the section where we will understand how support ministry can happen in a church in situations such as these redemption stories.

Basic Rules for Support Ministry

When I defended my Credo at seminary, the ethics professor caught me so off guard with his questions, but I will never forget how much I learned from his rigorous inquiry. He said, "Karen, in your Credo you talk about developing strategies and rules for people. But then when you talk about practical theology, you just talk about grace. How do you reconcile this difference? Do you act out of a rule-based system, or are you driven by grace?"

His question was so on target. I remember thinking, *This guy's really on to something.* I went into what I call "mother mode" for my response:

"My kids need rules. I need rules. But sometimes the rules don't work, and that is really the beauty of grace. We have to have the deontological approach (rule driven) for guidelines and direction; yet we also have to be teleological (grace-filled) for all of us to be redeemed."

Apparently the professor thought the answer had merit, because he passed me.

And that is what has to happen when you set up a support ministry of any type. People have to have guidelines. If you are the leader, you have to provide the rules and standards. That's the first step. As we all know, *rules are easy; grace is hard.*

So let's start with some basic rules for anyone in support ministry.

- Never allow yourself to be in an unsafe or compromising situation. One of the first things I asked for when I came to work at Resurrection was to have windows installed in our counseling room doors. Counselors, pastors, and volunteers need to understand that they are in positions of power when they are caring for someone. Three big rules include:

  1. Never set a "date" for a meal or coffee or travel with a person of the opposite sex with whom you are counseling.
  2. Never counsel someone alone in your church.
  3. Never go to a home visit alone if it may put you in a dangerous situation.

- Insist that all of your volunteers and staff take a course that teaches clear ethical boundaries set by your conference and denomination. If you are affiliated with a church that does not have such a course, most United Methodist churches can direct you to such a course. Our denominational course is called "Safe and Sacred Spaces." This course also allows the church to do a legal background check on those hoping to be certified.

- Teach and set standards for clothing for your staff and volunteers. When people are in a vulnerable situation, do not let your clothing detract from the sacred moments where you are entrusted to lead or counsel.

- Be aware of any sexual feelings that you might have for a congregant, staff member, colleague, volunteer, and so forth. Acknowledge these feelings to yourself. Debrief with someone safe and keep your feelings in check. Do not put yourself in a vulnerable position with them. Do not acknowledge these feelings to the person who is the object of these feelings.

- Keep your personal and family relationships healthy!

- Avoid burnout by taking your days off and finding ways to play.

- Pray and pay attention to the needs of your soul.

- Debrief and keep your own counsel with friends, preferably people not connected with your congregation.

- Find your own professional counselor.

These rules will be stretched and broken. Sometimes you have to gracefully encourage your staff, volunteers, or yourself to get back on course. But there are times when the rules are broken so badly that disciplinary action will need to be taken swiftly. Do not delay to seek help or counsel from a supervisor if the situation seems to be beyond what you can handle alone.

The young woman in the first story is ever so much wiser, and I'm sure she will never allow herself to be in a situation where she might be in jeopardy. She learned the lesson the hard way. Hopefully others can learn from the terrible offense her supervisor made and the choices that she made to trust him. But redemption happens when we share such stories. That young woman has now graduated from law school and will forever be an advocate for women. This is the power of redemption!

Volunteers Needed!

As you assess and prioritize the needs for your care ministry, decide who can help you set and attain your goals. No matter what the size of the church, your volunteers will be the lifeblood of your ministry. Staff is important, but to cultivate a trusted volunteer team will mean the difference in your church thriving or merely existing.

If someone says to you, "I would like to help you," begin to evaluate their gifts and graces. Before I had an assistant at Resurrection, I depended only on trusted volunteers who were in my office on Monday mornings attending to prayer concerns from the weekend while I did the hospital calls. Then they did the follow-up hospital calls, wrote notes, and made phone calls throughout the week. They also developed spreadsheets to list how, when, and who had given care. In addition, they helped me plan and execute special events such as healing services, baptism services, and special classes.

Fortunately, we are now at a point where each pastor has a dedicated, personal team of volunteers. We call our lay ministry team Congregational Care Ministers, or CCMs. They fill any number of roles in providing the best care for our congregation. Some are very relational and are quite capable of doing hospital visits, telephone calls, or sitting with people who need encouragement and prayer. Some of our CCMs have great administrative skills and provide amazing support help. Some CCMs may be professionally adept with finances, counseling, or medicine. We have been able to "employ and deploy" them in ways that utilize their skills. The CCMs enable us to provide a deeper level of care to our church family. Without the extra hands that CCMs provide, our care would be far less complete.

Selecting and Training Volunteers

Not every member of your congregation will have the gifts and skills necessary to fill this role of caring for the congregation. It is important to have processes in place for selection, training, and commissioning of new volunteers.

Some guidelines for selection include:

- A minimum term of membership to establish a deep connection to the church. We recommend three years;

- Regular worship attendance. Our guideline at Resurrection is that members attend weekly unless they are sick or out of town;

- Active pursuit of growth in the Christian life through participation in a small group or in some other form of Christian discipleship. We ask that our applicants take a year of study with our designated Bible course as well as another major teaching or leadership event within our church;

- Regular service to God with their time in the ministry of the church;

- Giving financially in proportion to their income with the tithe being the goal;

- Safe and Sacred Spaces or other type of certification to assure their understanding of boundaries.

In addition, each person who is interested in becoming a Congregational Care Minister is asked to fill out an application (see Appendix D), which asks for a spiritual biography. Following the application, interviews are conducted with a pastor and a staff member. Not all applicants will become CCMs. We try our best to direct people to other possibilities for volunteering where their unique gifts can be used best.

Once the volunteers are selected, we offer training in the fall and the spring that includes Praying Out Loud, Pastoral Care through Crisis, United Methodist Polity and Doctrine, Preparation of Sacred Spaces, Funerals and Weddings, Hospital Visitation, and Care for the Elderly. Other training that we provide includes four laity weekend classes at our local United Methodist seminary.

In January of each year we commission and honor our new CCMs. This is a big deal! We give each of them a certificate and introduce them to our congregation at every worship service. By publicly being given authority, CCMs will be much more able to do the duties that you assign them, as the congregation will understand that they truly are an extension of your office.

It is important that the pastor's confidence in the abilities of the CCMs is emphasized frequently during the first few months. Use the pulpit, use your newsletter, use classes you are leading, use whatever forum you have at your disposal. You may run into a mind-set of "If the senior pastor doesn't visit me, I haven't received good care," especially if the pastor has been the only person doing care visits. It is a great service to your volunteers and to your congregation to hear you affirm that your volunteers are qualified and trusted to provide quality care.

Once they are trained, our CCM teams meet regularly with their assigned pastor. However, the pastors call and connect with their CCMs every week to assign new duties and hear how assignments are going. We also provide a monthly meeting for all of our CCMs where they receive some sort of new training. Previous topics have included boundaries, counseling, member assistance, medical information, caring for the frail, dealing with dementia, and self-care.

I cannot stress to you enough the importance of using volunteers for this important ministry, because you cannot do this work alone. This model may not exactly fit your needs. But I hope that it gives you encouragement to develop a model that works for you, so when you go on vacation or eventually leave a congregation, these important people will carry on the legacy and standard of care that you have set. As you give them authority, the congregation will come to understand them to be the shepherds of the flock.

Pastoral Counseling

Many times, people in crisis will come first to their pastor because they hope to have a safe, confidential place to navigate a difficult situation. Remember as you take on this role that no one is expecting you to be the savior.

Are you ready? And I mean this seriously—are you ready spiritually to employ grace? This is where salvation can be offered.

As pastors and volunteers come into Congregational Care, it is helpful to have some guidelines and tools as you start into pastoral counseling.

First of all: Pray before each session. Get yourself in the right frame of mind that God really might work through you. Pray that your "stuff" will get out of the way and that the light of Christ might shine in you.

Ask the congregant to sign the appropriate paperwork. Our department has created paperwork that helps the congregant realize how much we respect the confidential nature of their situation. (Please see examples in Appendix F). When they first come into the office, I explain to them that everything we talk about is confidential, unless it needs to be shared with another pastor for ongoing ministry with them or with a psychological counselor. In both cases, I ask for them to give me clear authority to share. Also, if there is anything that might make me believe that they might be suicidal or might harm someone else, I tell them I am obligated by law to share the information with the appropriate people. In addition, all helping professionals are required to report child abuse. Your reporting requirements, as well as the limits of confidentiality, may vary according to your state laws. Please make sure you know these regulations and can communicate them, as needed, to persons seeking counseling.

Also inform the congregant about your own ethical boundaries, that usually as pastors we try to limit ourselves to four or five sessions with a congregant unless there is a very unusual circumstance. Such cases must be approved by the Senior or Executive Pastor. If you are the only pastor in your setting, this is a good time to confide in another clergy person, your counselor, or pastoral supervisor for guidelines on how to set healthy boundaries during long-term-care situations. I have found personally that issues of forgiveness may take longer, but what you can do is give the congregant the tools and then ask them to check back in a couple of months or refer them to a pastoral counselor or other trusted colleague.

To help them be ready to share, I explain that this is safe place and that I believe God heals through grace and not judgment, so I want them to be able to share without fear. At that point I offer a prayer something like this: "Gracious God, we thank you for the opportunity for John to share what is on his heart today. Allow him to dig deep and for me to listen with a heart that will not judge. Allow us to look together and to be alert to what you might be adding to this conversation. All this we pray in your Son's healing name. Amen."

Many times when I look up I see that the person is tearful and is ready to start down the healing journey.

Listen. This may seem like an easy task, but true listening takes skill and patience. Skilled pastors know how to ask leading questions and make reflective statements that will help the person open up. For instance, in a session that involves a marital problem, it is easy to begin with a very direct question: "Do both of you want this marriage to succeed?" This kind of question will allow both parties to hear the answer, and from there the story can begin to be told.

Do you see any signs of depression or mental illness that alarm you? Ask questions that will uncover symptoms of depression. How are you sleeping? How are you eating? Have you ever felt suicidal? Do you have a plan? It is critical for you as pastor to be ever vigilant of the dangers of wading into deeper waters where you don't have the skill level to be helpful. Be sure to find a mentor so you can debrief. Do not hesitate to seek psychological counseling for the person. There have been times during appointments in my office when a person has been suicidal and I have needed to take immediate action with the person's family. Keep a list with phone numbers of places and persons in your community that provide different kinds of help.

Offer sympathy. Allowing people to feel what they are feeling is important. Just having a safe place to express your feelings is a luxury. Sometimes as humans, we know that our feelings are shortsighted or contrary to where we'd like them to be. And what a gift it is to have someone simply acknowledge our humanness and be patient with us through our processing. Sometimes as people speak the words, it allows them to hear themselves and begin to move in a different direction. Just to have someone BE with you is a gift. Giving that gift as a pastor or skilled volunteer makes for a good day of ministry. Through just listening and being with someone, healing can begin to occur.

As you listen, be aware of your own feelings. These need not be shared with persons who are seeking help; however, your feelings are a clear signal about what is actually happening in the room between you. For example, if you typically find yourself feeling totally or unusually drained after meeting with a particular person, this may be an indication of how others also respond to him or her. There really are people who just wear us out, but your feelings may also indicate or be related to how empty that person feels. Another example is when you typically find yourself feeling bored or when the person is not really talking to you but to someone else—that is, you and the person just can't connect, which may be an indication that there are deeper psychological issues that may need to be addressed by a more seasoned counselor. You should also talk about your feelings with your own supervisor or counselor. If you have none available, consult with a respected and trusted colleague.

It is critical to look for subtle clues that might help you identify harmful situations where anger or sexuality issues may be a risk. There may also be family systems that you need to help uncover. Has there been a family history that bears out certain repeated behaviors? Does the person always try to manage everything?

One of the hardest things, I think, for people to consider is how to live in chaos or to wait until the right solution might be seen clearly. People usually want some sort of immediate direction.

Usually I find that they know the direction they should go; they just want you to affirm it or call it into question. WAIT for them to begin to reveal to you where they see the situation going. *After the story has been told,* allow time to reflect briefly on what you have heard. Do your best not to issue judgmental statements; let grace work. Allow the person to see mercy in your thinking so that they might model it. Sometimes there are no adequate words that you can find in response to their story, and it is OK to say just that: "Wow, I'm finding it hard to find words. Your situation is so difficult." This is rare; but believe me, when you think you have heard it all, someone will tell you something that is hard to comprehend. Moments when someone retells a story of traumatic death or childhood abuse are such times. When you hear such stories for the first time, you may feel completely unequipped to help. At these moments seek out mentors who can help you debrief and guide you for your next session.

A *pastoral response* is just that: pastoral. It is not psychological— there is a big difference.

If there are *theological questions,* I try to give biblical backup to my answers. (See Appendix B for suggested Scripture passages.) I might offer book suggestions that I have found helpful for their questions. I keep a short list on the subjects of grief, marriage, sexual abuse, addictions, and so forth. Although this list is by no means exhaustive, I have found these resources most helpful.

I always try to give the individual, couple, or family some "homework." It might be anything from memorizing a certain Scripture, attending worship, getting into a support group, going out on a date, creating a collage that tells their family story, or taking care of themselves in concrete ways.

Also know that I always keep a record of any Scripture, book, or homework that I have mentioned during my session with the congregants so that I can remember to ask them about it at our next session.

Some sessions really are not fun. Sometimes a session can be very difficult. People can become very frustrated or start digging into things that are very hurtful or scary as they remember them. Try your best to remain a listening presence, but do not allow their emotions to pull you into their drama. Sometimes this can be very difficult. A smart pastor realizes that most people aren't even aware of the mechanisms that they use to cope. Many times I have seen people go from being calm to tearful to angry within seconds. It is as if from childhood they have learned that this is the means to get their way or get their points advanced. Be alert to these methods. Help people grow by showing them other ways of communicating.

This is key: **The person must feel heard.** You need to understand how critical this is to them. Convey through your tone and body posture that they have your full attention.

Be very direct if you determine that they may be in a dangerous situation or suicidal: "Are you in a safe place right now?" "Is this the number where you can be reached?" "Is there anyone with you?" "Do you have a plan?"

If you feel there is danger of self-harm or of harming others, do not hesitate to call 911. There have been times when I have been on the line with someone who has been suicidal, and I have another person call 911. The person may be frustrated with you; but they will also appreciate that you were trying to do everything you could, especially when it may have meant life and death. Again remember there are legal reporting requirements about this.

We have developed a Safety and Self Care Contract (see Appendix H) for such situations. It can be useful to add accountability or to slow down or interrupt emotional responses. When both of you sign this document, a course of action becomes a concrete thing. Your signature is also a tangible sign to the congregant that you care about his or her well-being.

Anxiety can be contagious and can hijack your ability to provide good care. In difficult situations it is very important to manage your own anxiety. Do this by taking a deep breath, controlling your own tone, pace, response, and follow-up. Stop to pray if needed. This can break the cycle of anger, self-pity, or indecision that may be getting in the way of progress. Remember, you cannot control the response of the person you are in a session with, or other staff members' responses, or the outcome.

Also remember that you are in control of the session length. So generally it is best to say from the onset that you have set aside, perhaps, an hour. The greater clarity you can give, the better it usually is. Setting boundaries in space (a quiet, safe place) and time (decided ahead of time) gives persons a sense of structure and will help them better manage their anxiety. It will also help you as well. Note that the Counseling Intake Paperwork form in Appendix F clearly states that the session will be limited to an hour.

Allow yourself grace when dealing with complex or emotionally difficult counseling situations. Remember, when we get down "into the dirt" with people as Jesus did with the woman in John 8, it can be very difficult. Do not be discouraged. Find a colleague, supervisor, or counselor to help you process your feelings and to offer you advice.

Last, offer comfort. The Scriptures tell us, "Do not leave them comfortless." What does this mean? Always offer a next step for those who come to see you, even if it is just seeing them in worship next week. They have come to you and spilled their story. They have offered you a part of their life that perhaps no one else has ever heard. You are acting on behalf of Christ and the church. What would Christ do for this lamb? Ask yourself hard questions about your care.

Let's reflect quickly on the case studies for the chapter:

Redemption Story 1: The woman assaulted by her supervisor

Many women in such situations have a difficult time identifying abuse when it is happening. Often the behavior intensifies so gradually that it may not seem inappropriate until it has gone too far. Predators will take advantage of people of any age and most predators do not realize their own sickness until they are called on it in a big way.

In this particular instance, the young woman was so full of shame that it was clear we needed to pray about her own need of grace. The theological story of grace is made clear in Romans 5–8, which ends with the assurance that nothing will be able to separate us from the love of God in Christ Jesus our Lord.

If you can slowly work your way through these chapters and speak to the hope that is found in the journey of justification through grace, you will be able to help the congregant own the idea of salvation in a whole new way. Sometimes the words of Scripture do not mean anything to us until they come alive in our own story. Then we understand the need for a savior.

The young woman had several sessions with me as we talked about grace and justice. But also very important to her journey was the need for a psychological counselor. She was receiving both psychological and spiritual counsel that I truly believe helped her, and now she will be able to do likewise for others in her life.

Redemption Story 2: The couple dealing with infidelity

This particular case offered lots of opportunity for a study in forgiveness. Sessions that work on forgiveness, especially in cases of infidelity, can be full of ups and downs. But again, if you model grace and give the couple guidelines to grace, you can help them see a new Christlike way.

Guidelines for Grace:

GIVE plenty of space to the people in the situation.

RESPOND instead of react.

ACCESS the big picture of the situation.

CONCENTRATE on Bible verses that ground you.

ENCOURAGE each other on the journey and **be patient with the process.**

John was very repentant, which was a great help in the healing process. Even years later, he is still working on his redemption. It was important for him to realize that this will probably be a lifelong process, but this journey can bring the couple to a wonderful new place in their relationship that could only be a God-given gift.

Redemption Story 3: The young woman struggling with alcohol and depression

Because Cindy's life ended with suicide, there is a need for God's grace to be spoken into the situation.

The following are some helpful ideas for comforting the family:

• God is weeping also.

- There is no condemnation in suicide. God, who is the great parent, would have hoped for a long life for the person, but the evils (drugs or alcoholism or mental health issues) of the world were working against the person.

- Imagine the person with a new body, free from the pain they were experiencing.

- Find ways to honor the person with service work, and so forth.

- It is important to note that the family usually will have guilt issues that can be very painful for a time.

Again, practice the guidelines of grace as you minister to the family.

As you might suspect, this case was also difficult for me.

To end this section on counseling, please see Appendix I, which includes care guidelines for several different life situations. It will give you signs to look for, talking points, Scriptures, suggested reading, and resources for different topics. You may find it helpful to build your own index for potential counseling calls.

What a gift it is to be a healer for God in this very personal way. My prayer for you is that it blesses you deeply as you care for others.

Oh, sweet redemption!

Classes and Groups

As you continue to explore ways to care for your congregation, you may have people approach you about starting a group experience. We are constantly assessing the current needs of the congregation, and sometimes it can be very helpful to address situations in such a way. Out of my experience, I have found that group ministry can be very beneficial for several reasons:

- Common experiences can provide for empathetic responses.

- Groups can provide time to teach curriculum to large numbers of people.

- People can learn appropriate responses from others.

- It can be a very time-saving way to do ministry with people who are facing similar situations.

How you do group ministry is so important. I'd like to share a few important tips that we have learned.

First, try your group as a class instead of as a support group. I have found this to be an effective way to gauge the interest of the group. There is a great advantage in having a start date and an end date to the group as opposed to not having an end date, which may be the case with a support group. Sometimes support groups can become unhealthy as people are allowed to linger in their situation instead of graduating and moving on.

Second, make sure you have good facilitators who are skilled at leading such a group. Set standards for them, such as checking in with you at least once a month through an e-mail or a debriefing session.

Help your leaders develop a curriculum that begins and ends with prayer, includes handouts, and has a definite spiritual component. People can find great secular resources outside the church, but most of the time they are coming to church to receive something they could not receive elsewhere. For instance, many hospitals provide grief care, but by coming to a church, the expectation is that there will be a spiritual component. Many counselors provide support groups for those going through divorce, but a divorce recovery group at a church should include a very nonjudgmental faith approach. The question to ask yourself is, "How does this group offered at the church differ from one offered in the community?"

Once you decide to have a course, publicize it in your usual ways and issue targeted invitations to those who might be interested. Go through your lists of recent funerals to target potential members of a grief class, keep your ears open for recent or difficult divorce situations, notice if there is an increase in parenting challenges or if your community is especially hard hit by a slow economy, and so forth. You want your efforts to pay off. The point is that these classes and groups must address the needs of YOUR community. If the class experience is good, you may want to make it into a regular support group. But again, I would be cautious about calling it a support group, as it really does imply that there is a long-term commitment.

If you decide to move forward with forming a support group, you might want to create a standard process for determining the need and appropriateness of this new ministry. Our process includes asking questions designed to help those who are proposing the support group:

1. What is the purpose of the proposed ministry? What does God want to accomplish with the proposed ministry? Describe how this is in accord with Resurrection's purpose statement: "to build a Christian community where nonreligious and nominally-religious people are becoming deeply committed Christians."

2. Who will the new ministry serve? Who is the primary audience for this ministry? Who will it benefit or serve?

3. Which needs will the new ministry meet? Consider spiritual, physical, emotional, intellectual, and relational needs.

4. What services will the new ministry offer? What kinds of services will the ministry provide for these needs?

5. How will we provide these services? What will be the ministry strategy for providing services? What will be the operational plan? What is the process?

6. Describe the leadership structure that the new ministry will require. What are the various roles and ministry responsibilities that are needed to support this ministry? Describe the proposed structure of the ministry.

7. What kinds of resources will the new ministry require? Consider training, support services, facilities, computer access, mailboxes, assistance of church staff, finances, announcements, and the like.

8. What is the vision for growth and expansion? What growth is expected? What is the "dream" for this ministry two years from now?

9. How will the effectiveness of this ministry be evaluated? Include measurement systems that will gauge whether the ministry is successful in accomplishing its purpose.

10. Does this ministry already exist in the church? Is there similarity between this ministry and one that your church already offers? Should it be coordinated with other ministries? Should it replace an existing ministry?

The answers to these questions form the plan for the support group. Lay leaders are champions of such efforts. It is always important, though, to offer a chance for regular debriefing with the leaders: encourage and praise them in their efforts. What a gift to have a strong support ministry to help weather the storms of life and to aid in the redemption process.

As we close this chapter on support ministries, I want to encourage you again to continually assess your congregation and community. There may be some great ministries ready to be born as you try to address ever-changing needs.

It is vital that we stay alert, nimble, adaptable, and grounded in our own spiritual lives in order to be effective in ministry.

Questions for Reflection

Who would you contact regarding ethical issues?

Do you understand the legalities of pastoral responsibility?

Do you have clear personal boundaries?

- Do you make it clear to a congregant what those boundaries are?

Do you maintain personal space during appointments?

- Is your office furniture set up to create a space that maintains boundaries?

- Is there a window in your door?

Do you know what types of behaviors must be reported to the authorities?

- To church authorities?

- To law enforcement agencies such as child or elder protective offices or the police?

- Do you know what steps to take to make a report?

Have you ever utilized a personal counselor during especially stressful seasons?

- Can you debrief with fellow clergy?

- Is there someone to whom you are not related or a nonparishioner in whom you can confide?

Consider how rules + grace = redemption.

- When have you experienced redemption as a result of the two (rules and grace) together?

- Have you seen redemption happen with only grace or with only rules?

CHAPTER THREE

The Most Sacred Hours: Caring for the Sick

*Is any one of you in trouble? He should pray. Is anyone
happy? Let him sing songs of praise. Is any one of you
sick? He should call the elders of the church to pray over
him and anoint him with oil in the name of the Lord.
And the prayer offered in faith will make the sick person
well; the Lord will raise him up.*
—*James 5:13-15 NIV*

The pager call came on a Sunday regarding the illness of a
middle-aged wife and mother of three adolescent children.
Lisa was her name. The day before, she had had a seizure and
blacked out. Lisa, who was also a pediatric nurse practitioner,
quickly realized that she needed help. She was hospitalized and
an MRI was done with frightening results: a brain tumor.

This was all I knew when I walked into a hospital room full of
family. I remember meeting Lisa's mother and dad, her husband,
sister, and three children. But hanging in the room was the question we all sensed: "What next?"

On that first visit, Lisa seemed relieved and glad to see someone from church; likewise the mother and dad were also relieved. Although the others welcomed me, I just remember seeing fear in their eyes. They told me that there would be more tests in the next few days to discover the type of cancer. That afternoon, we read Scripture to help calm the anxiety (1 Peter 5:7-11); then I anointed Lisa and prayed for complete healing and relief from fear.

How does redemption or restoration happen through such a situation? In this chapter we will explore how great care can happen while navigating the pitfalls of a dreadful diagnosis.

Hospital Visits

Hospital visitation is one of the most important elements of care that can be offered through the church. As pastors and volunteers of care attempt to do this type of ministry with skilled eyes and intui-tive hearts, we should understand the multiple dimensions of our being human that are closely intertwined. When the body is affected, spiritual and psychological well-being can also be affected. Plus, when one person is hurting, that person's family and friends may also need care. It is important to note up front that we need to attend to the family and friends of the sick. *It is so important that the pastor or volunteer be sensitive to the implications of physical change or pain. It is complex ministry and must always be bathed in prayer.*

Because of the complexity of demands upon any pastor or pastoral staff, care can best be accomplished through a **team effort**. We have educated our congregation and staff to follow clear lines of care that are similar to a medical model of calling your doctor.

The congregation can contact the church for care for the sick through three usual methods: (1) a call to our office; (2) a prayer request card that is usually received through the offering plates; and (3) a call to the pager, which in our case is rotated among the pastors. All these requests for care for the sick go to one central place or person on staff who will triage the intake and deploy the caregivers. This person's position is extremely important, be it a staff person or volunteer, because of the volume of care and the need to keep track of each person.

Again I want to emphasize: *communicate clearly to your congregation their responsibility to get information to you for this important ministry.* By doing this primary work, you will be able to give more complete care to the congregation.

Once the church has been notified about a need for care, the triage person can find out the hospital or surgical date, time, and place as well as the congregant's relationship to the church. Also needed are contact information and the reason for admission, should the patient want it to be given. Once this information is obtained, it is stored electronically, handwritten on a central calendar, and posted on a calendar whiteboard (which is seen only by pastoral staff).

For an emergency need, the pastor is notified so an immediate visit can be made. If the pastor cannot go, a key volunteer (CCM) is deployed. This procedure is for the weekday routine, but over the weekend, it is important to give your congregation a way that they can access care. The usual means are through a cell phone or a pager contact that is listed publicly, for example, in the Sunday morning bulletin, website, or newsletter.

Once the initial visit is made, two actions should follow: (1) *documentation of the visit*, including information gathered about the illness, those persons who were present, and the care that was given (anointing, Scripture, and prayer) and (2) *a suggested plan for follow-up care*. This information should be given back to the triage person who can create *the follow-up care plan*. For all practical purposes, the pastor should always be informed of important changes. Also, it is important to let the family or individual know what the next steps will be in your care.

Special considerations should be assessed in each situation, but the following are factors: age of the patient, severity of the illness, intensive care situation, possibility of imminent death, prolonged illness, involvement of other churches, family situation, and so forth.

Here are some important guidelines you might consider for your church:

- If the patient is a child, daily contact should be made by a volunteer or staff, and the pastor should set a personal standard of visiting at least two times a week.

- If the patient is in intensive care or it is a critical case, the pastor or volunteer should visit every day.

- If there is an imminent death, the pastor should visit and assess the situation.

- If the patient has a prolonged illness, a volunteer provides follow-up care as the pastor assigns.

- If a patient is dying, or has died, this is of utmost concern and urgency. When death occurs, the pastor is to be notified ASAP and attend to the family immediately. If the church office is notified of the death by a pager call, the pastor or the volunteer who is on call is to go immediately to the family.

Important Elements of a Hospital Call

Begin with the basics. Learn where to park at the hospitals near you. Make sure you have your "hospital kit": your Bible (I keep mine in the car), anointing oil, business cards, and a small supply of appropriate gifts. Suggestions for gifts include: prayer shawls, lap quilts, a small Bible with special verses marked, or small devotional books. You may want to enlist people in your congregation to make or help put these gifts together in a special way. You may want to include the church name and contact information.

Bring a nametag and wear it so that your intentions are clear to the hospital staff, the patient you are visiting, as well as any family members. Your nametag will also avoid any awkwardness the family or staff may feel if they don't know your name.

Also, if you, the pastor, feel the need to share Communion or baptize someone, make sure you have prepared the elements. Have fresh juice and bread. "Prepare the table" in the room with great respect. You can purchase a small communion set for such situations or use prepackaged juice and wafer combinations. Take a small, clean cloth to put under the elements as you set them up on the bedside table. Make it a sacred space for the sacrament you are making available. If the patient is unable to ingest the elements, ask the nurse for a mouth swab to dab juice on the tongue and break off a tiny piece of bread for a small taste. Always make sure you have washed your hands before and after you serve Communion.

If volunteers take Communion to a patient, instruct them and discuss how the pastor can consecrate the elements.

If you know you may be asked to perform a baptism, be prepared with a small bowl for water. Some pastors also use anointing oil to anoint for healing. If the person to be baptized is a child who may not live, be sure that you are prepared to ask appropriate questions of the parents and family. It will not be the usual "Will you promise to raise this child in the body of believers?" Be prepared to say something such as, "Will you promise to love and nurture this child that he or she might understand the love of God through your care?" This leaves it more open-ended. If the child lives, they will raise him or her in the body of believers; if the child dies, they will feel good about their promise to love the child as any devoted Christian parent would. The key here is to be very sensitive and very PREPARED.

Many pastors and volunteers feel at home and at ease in a hospital or nursing home setting. If you do not, or you sense that someone you are working with is not comfortable in a medical setting, you may need to find ways to overcome your fears or aversions. Be patient with yourself and usually you will find that in time, the sights, sounds, smells, hallways, and rooms become more familiar and thus lose their fright factor. I want to encourage you to keep trying and make this a personal goal, as I truly believe this is one of the most sacred places for a pastor or volunteer to be. Life-and-death issues are common here. Incredible ministry is possible in this setting. People in a hospital need the message of the gospel that you are bringing.

If the situation is critical and you must do ministry in an emergency room with family and friends, it may be helpful to take along a colleague to help or to contact the hospital chaplain (if available) ahead of time. As you practice ministry in your town, you will get to know the hospital chaplains who can help you understand immensely the situation you are about to encounter. Many hospitals also have special places to speak with family members privately and some have chapels that are open for prayer and even services.

How to Have a Successful Hospital Call

Now let me walk you through some of the basics about a successful hospital call.

First, make sure you have permission to visit. There are times when the patient or family does not want any visitors except the immediate family. Most of the time, a visitor from their faith community is appreciated, but out of courtesy it is important to make sure you are welcome. If family or friends are present, ask before you assume that it is a good time to visit. Most of the time people are glad to see someone representing their church.

Before you go into the room, pause to pray that God will use you to offer comfort and hope. Remember that your role is to be the hands and feet of Christ on earth. Have a passage of Scripture in mind that might be helpful during the visit.

The pastor or volunteer making the call should go into the room with a spirit of concern and encouragement. Remember your "kit": Bible, anointing oil, business cards, gifts, and the like.

Introduce yourself and your role, especially for those you do not know.

If the person is in a wheelchair or chair, try your best to be at eye level to them. If they are in bed, *do not* sit on the bed. You can sit in a chair if one is close by and you ask their permission. In the hospital, people find themselves feeling very powerless. Your asking their permission empowers them and allows them to be assured of your sensitivity to their situation.

Ask how they are doing today. If you have not received information about the nature of their illness, it is good to ask the question. If they called the church, they want you to know (assuring confidentiality) that you might be able to pray specifically about their situation.

Here are some other questions that may be helpful: How long have you been affiliated with the church? Are you involved with anything at church (Sunday school class, small group, family involvement, and so forth)? Find out what support systems they have. Do they have any family or friends in the area? If you have known the person for a while, it may be comforting for you to call up memories of more normal times together.

LISTEN to their story. Ask open-ended questions that relate to the person's needs. You do not need to relay any personal story of your own suffering or talk about someone else you know who had the same illness the patient has. As the pastor or minister from the church, help them remember their faith and that God loves them. This is what the patient really wants. It may surprise you that many patients feel that God has abandoned them or is punishing them for some wrongdoing. Remind them of the hope and healing that God wants for them. Remind them of God's steadfast concern for their well-being.

READING SCRIPTURES of hope and release from fear or anxiety are always appropriate.

After ample sharing has occurred, tell the patient you would like to PRAY FOR THEM. Ask: "What would you like me to pray?" Let them explain fully.

Then ask if you may ANOINT them before you pray. Remind them that the Scriptures tell us to anoint as we pray for healing. James 5:14 says, "Are any among you sick? They should call for the elders of the church and have them pray over them, anointing them with oil in the name of the Lord." If family is present, include them in the conversation and, of course, the prayer. Almost always, I recommend praying for complete healing and release from any fears or anxieties they might have.

At the end of the visit, give the patient your business card and let him or her know that he or she can call the church if any other care is needed. Also, let them know when they can expect another visit from the church and who might be coming. All this information allows the patient to know that you're going to be walking along beside them during this experience.

If your church has a ministry that helps provide food for the family or when the patient returns home, you can discuss that as well.

If the patient is asleep or out of the room for procedures when you stopped by, leave your card to let the patient and family know that you were there. If the patient is not available, pray before you leave the room and leave a note indicating that you have prayed for them. Sometimes the gift of a prayer shawl, pocket Testament, or quilt offer ongoing comfort.

If you have ever been hospitalized or had surgery, you will understand that this is a sacred time for individuals and their families. As pastors and care volunteers, we are allowed to see and be with people at vulnerable moments. I would encourage you to cherish this time. It is precious, because these moments of ministry will be remembered for years.

Special Elements and Situations

In the United Methodist tradition, anointing with oil offers an opportunity for spiritual healing as affirmed by Scripture in James 5:13-15. This prayer of faith says, "Is any one of you in trouble? He should pray. Is anyone happy? Let him sing songs of praise. Is any one of you sick? He should call the elders of the church to pray over him and anoint him with oil in the name of the Lord. And the prayer offered in faith will make the sick person well; the Lord will raise him up" (NIV).

The United Methodist Book of Worship explains that "anointing the forehead with oil is a significant act invoking the healing love of God. The oil points beyond itself and those doing the anointing to the action of the Holy Spirit and the presence of the healing Christ, who is God's Anointed One." (See *The United Methodist Book of Worship* [Nashville: The United Methodist Publishing House, 1992].)

Anointing gives the opportunity for spiritual healing, which is a wholeness of body, mind, and spirit. The oil reminds us of God's promise of presence with those who are sick or suffering. Anointing offers the *healing* of being made whole in the love of Christ rather than the physical *cure* of illness.

Anointing people who are frail is a powerful reminder of God's triune presence in their journey, offering them assurance that they do not travel alone and helping complete their circle of faith at the end of life. We anoint at baptism and near the completion of life.

When anointing someone:

1. Explain anointing and get permission (or the permission of family present).

The person may not be familiar with anointing in the United Methodist tradition. Explain what it is and how you will do it. Ask the person if this is something he or she would like to experience.

2. Read the passage from James 5:13-15 if it seems appropriate.

After reading the Scripture passage, remind the person that the anointing is not offered as a *cure*, but instead as inviting the

Holy Spirit to be present with them, offering wholeness in the love of Christ.

3. Anoint with oil in the name of the Father, Son, and Holy Spirit.

With anointing oil on the thumb, make the sign of the cross on the person's forehead, saying, "I anoint you with oil in the name of the Father, Son, and Holy Spirit."

4. You may want to pray the Lord's Prayer.

5. Finish by reading Psalm 23.

One way to conclude is by reading Psalm 23, reminding the person that God walks with us *through* our valleys, our dark times.

If death is imminent: another special concern is when it is a terminal situation. There are usually two distinct ways this journey can occur: a quick death or a long illness. If death is imminent, make sure that you communicate to the family a sense of calm and assurance about the outcome. As Christians, we should have no doubt of eternity's promise, and as the person is near death, we can create a bridge to heaven. This is the essence of ministry as death nears.

When the family calls the church and you know it may happen that day, there are some key ways to help the family and the loved one get to a sense of peace. Let me explain.

- Picture the time when the hour is near for the person who is dying.

- Have the family circle around the bedside.

- Begin with the idea that this is a very sacred hour. They have run the race and their most important people are gathered around the bedside to send them off to heaven. Even if the person seems comatose,

I speak as if that person is hearing every word I say. I have had experiences in which the person nearing death will rally for one last word. Just assume they don't want to miss a word of what you are saying. Usher in peace and calm with your presence.

There are key Scriptures that you can use.

First: Revelation 21:1-5 (a new heaven and a new earth). Many times, I'll begin by explaining what we believe as Christians and what that person is about ready to experience. I do this by reading from Revelation that Jesus is on the throne, the old has passed away, and God is about ready to make all things new. Even if they cannot respond, I ask the person if they've already begun to see visions of heaven or who has gone on before them who will be there to greet them.

Next: I read 1 Corinthians 15:51-57 (Where, O death, is your victory?) and explain what it might be like to leave this reality. In terms that everyone can comprehend, I talk about how death is like taking off an old coat that is completely used up and that God has prepared a new garment for us. This new body is perfect and pain-free.

Then: I move on to John 14:1-6a (Do not let your hearts be troubled.) I ask the family what kind of place they think God has prepared for the person. Do they like certain foods, or colors, or do they like to be at the beach? God has something absolutely perfect waiting for them.

Last: I take the family to Romans 8:38-39 and confirm that "nothing can separate us from the love of Christ," and ending with, "For I am convinced that neither death, nor life, nor angels, nor rulers, nor things present, nor things to come, nor powers, nor height, nor depth, nor anything else in all creation, will be able to separate us from the love of God in Christ Jesus our Lord." Assure the person with a sentence that the loved one will be with God and even as they close this chapter, they will be reunited.

Right after this Scripture, I move quickly to anointing the person and closing with prayer.

I pray for the time ahead to be filled with sacred moments for the family, comfort for everyone, decreased pain, and God's perfect timing. We thank God for the person and at the end of this prayer I close either with the Lord's Prayer or the Twenty-third Psalm. After this, I give the family my contact information and let them know when we can plan on talking again. The family needs to know what to expect from you and their church. They are feeling powerless and this knowledge allows them to know how you are going to walk them through this. Most people go through this only a few times in their life, and it is so important to be there as a church during these sacred hours.

If the prognosis is for a longer journey, it is important to create a team of people who can attend to the person. One way to do this is to create with the patient a timeline of important events ahead for them. Are they going through chemotherapy? How often will the treatments be? Do they have surgery ahead of them? Are there particular people they are worried about? Are there tasks that they feel need to be completed? Are there people with whom they need to make peace? Is there a funeral plan in place? Do they have a Do Not Resuscitate document? Are medical and legal durable powers of attorney in place?

Whether or not the outcome will be life or death, all of these questions are important for the person on this long journey. Sometimes they do not even know how to articulate these questions. One very important document that you can use to help the person with all these questions is called *Caring Conversations*. It is in booklet form and can be accessed on line at www.practical bioethics.org.

When the timing is right, introduce the person to Caring Conversations. Tell them you're just going to give it to them, and that the next time you visit you will work through it with them. Allow them time to digest and ponder these important questions.

In the case of Lisa (see the very beginning of this chapter), she used this document to attend to tasks that she knew would be important. Sometimes when she felt up to it, we had long conversations about the children, her husband, sister, parents, and career friends. In addition, we had tough theological conversations.

Theological Conversation

My visiting Lisa brought up her concerns about God. Our theological conversations went along the lines that you might expect. She wanted to know, *Why me, God?*

One day Lisa called my office and asked if I could come over. It was springtime, and I remember sitting outside in the family's beautiful backyard. Lisa said she was just angry that day. Why me, God? And although Lisa was theologically savvy and pretty much knew what answer I would give her, she just needed to step through the process to get past her anger. She had read *The Will of God* by Leslie Weatherhead and *When Bad Things Happen to Good People* by Rabbi Harold Kushner, so she had already sought answers that way. She understood that life is not fair and that our bodies are fragile. She had been at the bedsides when children had died. So she had the "head knowledge" of life and death. But no matter who we are, we will have our moment when the questions belong to us in a profoundly personal way. And it is at that moment when we need to have someone walk through the process with us. Confusion, anger, and hurt are allowed, but we don't want to get stuck there. So we wrestle with the questions and help people move forward. But I have also seen people get stuck on the "Why me?" question, turn inward, and become completely self-absorbed, pushing friends and family away. For these people, their final days can become a pity party. However, I've seen a lot more people wrestle with the hard questions and even pain, yet go on to end well, cradled in the love and care of companions and even staff. As caregivers, we are called to guide people so that these last hours can be sacred.

One particular sacred hour that I will never forget with Lisa was when she was nearing the end of her journey. Her middle child, John, had suddenly become reluctant to go close to his mother's bed. Lisa had her sister call me. I knelt beside her bed as she asked me to try to get her son to come in to see her.

John was out in the living room watching TV. It really did not take any more than a simple invitation: "Would you like to go with me to read some Scripture and pray with your mom?" He jumped up and said, "Sure." My hunch was that he just didn't know what to do in the space alone.

This is a typical response many people have in the face of this great unknown. They want you, as a pastor or a spiritual guide, to lead them into the space where death is close. Once we were there, it was this wonderful, sacred moment. The twelve-year-old boy snuggled in with his mom as I knelt beside them and recited some verses of Scripture in the dimly lit room. After reading the Scripture, I prayed for God's holy peace and comfort to saturate the room. Then I said my good-bye for the day and said I'd call the next day.

This was a redeeming moment: a sacred moment of restoring the close relationship for both of them.

Questions and Reflections

What is in your hospital kit? Where do you keep it?
Do you have key phrases, prayers, and Scripture texts to use for:

- Someone about to go into surgery?

- Someone who has received a diagnosis of a serious illness?

- Someone with a terminal illness?

- At someone's bedside when death is imminent or has recently occurred?

- Regular visits to someone in a long-term care facility?

How do you personally feel about anointing?

- Have you experienced it?

- How did it make you feel?

- Is this something you can share with your congregation?

- How can you introduce your congregation to it?

- How will you use it in your ministry setting?

Can you cite an example of redemption happening for a person with a chronic or terminal illness?

CHAPTER FOUR

Leading Through the Valley of the Shadow of Death

The LORD is my shepherd, I shall not want.
    He makes me lie down in green pastures;
he leads me beside still waters;
    he restores my soul.
He leads me in right paths
    for his name's sake.

Even though I walk through the darkest valley,
    I fear no evil;
for you are with me;
        your rod and your staff—
        they comfort me.

You prepare a table before me
    in the presence of my enemies;
you anoint my head with oil;
    my cup overflows.
Surely goodness and mercy shall follow me
    all the days of my life,
and I shall dwell in the house of the LORD
    my whole life long.

—Psalm 23

You only bury your mother once.

Heaven forbid that you'd have to bury your child.

Yet when you are a pastor, you will have to lead people through these events many times in your career. I am convinced that there is no greater service that you can give a family than to lead them through this valley. In fact, I believe that death trumps every other element of pastoral ministry. It is the greatest fear that most people face. But it is the gift of Jesus' life that he conquered the grave: "Death, where is your sting?"

As you lead people through this important valley, you will discover that moments of redemption happen in many ways. As people gather, the petty grievances can disappear if there is good leadership. You can actually help dysfunctional families if they are open. I have seen relationships restored over and over again. Christ came to make these moments of redemption possible. Your coming to minister during these difficult times helps people experience these moments for themselves as individuals and sometimes as a community.

With that idea, let's continue with the story of Lisa's family that I began in Chapter 3. Lisa had been transferred to a nearby hospice house as her condition worsened. Daily visits were a part of my routine. However, there came a three-day stretch when I was going to be out of town for a conference. Late Tuesday night of the conference, I received a call from Lisa's husband, Kevin. He left a voice message, and I could tell from the sound of his voice that the end had come. I called back and quickly told them I'd return first thing in the morning. This meant changing my airline flight, but at that moment, they were counting on the fact that someone would show up and lead them through this. During these hours they had to be reassured that death does not have the last word.

The key here is readiness: readiness for the family and readiness to have others step in if you are absent. As you do your daily visit, it is so important to help the family be ready for the event. Just as an expectant mother takes birthing classes, you should walk this journey with the family, be alert to where they are, and gradually open their hearts and minds to the peace that is possible. You will often encounter a resistant member of the family whose anger, denial, and frustration holds them back. The quicker you can interact with them, and faithfully keep reminding them that this is not the end, the greater the chance of an amazing, sacred death experience.

I was able to change my flight to be at Lisa's bedside, but there will be times when you simply cannot be present. Readiness must also be part of the journey as you bring another key layperson or pastor into the picture just in case you are not immediately available when the moment of death happens. One pastor stated it so clearly: "Jesus must show up." And that happens as we represent the hands, feet, voice, and presence of the living Lord.

Do not assume that a brief prayer over the phone is adequate. You must GO.

Whether at the home or the hospital, a calming presence is key. Probably the best response is first to just say, "I'm so sorry." No matter what the age or circumstances, the family feels an immense loss. If the body is still present, you might ask if you may anoint the deceased. Do so without hesitation. The body is not to be feared. As you do the anointing, you can pray with thanksgiving for the ways that this person served with their hands (anoint hands) or their feet (anoint feet).

This anointing of the body is biblical and extends a wonderful holiness that both dispels fears and creates a holy service. You may want to create a small bedside service in bulletin form to use in such a situation. You can keep copies of it in your car. If the person is in a facility such as a hospital, hospice house, or care center, you may want to invite the staff as they certainly will have their moments of grief. Do not be shy about inviting the staff. They will feel the loss as surely as the family does, and this is a powerful moment of ministry to them as well.

Try to assess the needs of the different people present. Spend as much time as needed. The family is looking to you to provide prayer, Scriptures of God's promises, and words of comfort. The sacred moments around a body can be especially important for the family as this is a moment as Christians when our hope in Christ is affirmed.

After everyone has been cared for and before you leave, make a plan with the responsible family or friends. It is best if you can wait until the mortuary comes for the body; then you can talk about next steps. Give the family your business card, noting e-mail and phone numbers where you can be reached. If possible, agree on a time when you or the pastor might be able to meet with the family to plan the service if needed.

Always exit with a prayer and words of comfort.

Funeral Planning

Planning a funeral service is one of the most important elements of care that a pastor can ever do for a family. Although funeral planning is usually reserved for the pastor, there are also many opportunities for volunteers to help care for the family, for example, providing food, transportation, care of children, and care of pets. Amazing moments of redemption and restoration can happen.

One such story was with a family I had known for many years. I officiated at their daughter's wedding, I taught their Bible classes, and I was there as the matriarch prepared to die. Another pastor and I walked the long journey with the family. The elderly mother had three children, two boys and one daughter. Rita, the wife of the elder son, Mike, was the main caregiver, and it had not been an easy journey for her. For over a year, Rita and Mike had Mike's mother living with them. Rita felt as if nothing she did ever satisfied her mother-in-law. So when the time of death came and all of the family had gathered for the meeting, everyone gave their individual stories that reflected a mother who was funny, thoughtful, and loved. All except for Rita, who did not say anything for over an hour. At this point, I asked Rita if she'd like to offer some stories about her mother-in-law.

She was very hesitant to speak but gradually came forth with her confession that she did not have the same feelings: "I had a different experience." As Rita shared her feelings, it provided the other family members with a wonderful opportunity that they grabbed without hesitation. I can remember the brother-in-law saying over and over how thankful they were for all that Rita had sacrificed and done for the entire family. They recognized that it was not easy. Others around the circle followed suit. This was a major turning point for the family—a moment of redemption for all. From that time on, there was renewed openness and trust. The conversation never turned sour, and it was healing for all present. Some even confessed that they felt they had done less than they might have. Others confessed to feeling inadequate. And with every confession, there was someone else saying, "It is OK; you did good."

These beautiful moments of restoration were such a gift to the family. When we left that night, over two hours after we started, the eldest son thanked the other pastor and me over and over saying that their family could not have imagined how such a seemingly difficult meeting could have been made so wonderful.

In preparation for such a meeting, encourage the family to have everyone present who would want to help plan the service. Identify a family spokesperson. Take your Bible and hymnal. Once you get to the house, take a deep breath and pray in order to center yourself. When you enter the home, introduce yourself and try your best to get the names of everyone present and the relationship to the deceased.

At this moment, they are waiting for you to lead. They are counting on you to take charge and help them go through this awkward, unknown "valley of the shadow."

When you enter into such a meeting, express to the family that you are honored and humbled to be a part of this very sacred time for them. Explain to them that you have three purposes in mind:

- to honor their loved one

- to care for them

- to plan a service of worship and give thanks to God.

Once you have said these three things, invite them to pray.

If you are able to set up in this way, they will begin to relax and trust that you know how to lead them through this time.

You might find that it is useful to prepare a worksheet that helps you collect the information for the service. This might include, but is not limited to, the following:

- significant life events of the deceased

- significance to others

- important adjectives that describe the person with stories to illustrate those traits

- faith story for the deceased

- requested Scripture (be prepared with Scriptures that you think might fit)

- requested music (be prepared to offer music suggestions)

You may want to show them a funeral bulletin of a service that you have previously officiated.

Important questions about logistics might include:

- When and where they'd like to hold the service. Invite them to use your church even if they are not members. This is a great evangelistic tool!

- Which mortuary did they choose?

- How many people might be expected at the service?

- Does anyone have special needs?

- Is there is to be a graveside service? Do family members want to speak there? Are there special requests?

Many times a family will say they'd like to have two or three people in addition to the pastor speak at the service. I encourage you to state very early in the conversation your experience in this regard. Explain to them that you would be glad to take all of their comments (written or spoken) and weave them into a eulogy.

And speaking from experience, I encourage you as pastor to tell them that you have found that it can really be a mistake to have someone other than the pastor try to speak during the service. Many times people break down or say things that are not helpful. You can tell them that you have found that the best time to have "an open microphone" is at a gathering afterward. Invite them to think this over carefully. Remind them that people are very vulnerable and that mourning can take many forms. Sharing together in a more conducive atmosphere can help the grieving process begin to move toward healing. Sharing can make for a wonderful time of celebration, because often families and friends are together who may not have seen each other for years.

However, if the family insists that they would like to have others speak at the service, set a limit on how many can speak: a good rule of thumb is no more than two. Agree on the length of time each person will speak, usually no more than three to five minutes. Then tell them you'd like to meet with the person(s) to make sure there will not be any repetition in the stories and so that you all can walk through the order of service to ensure that it will go smoothly. At your meeting, be sure to tell those who are going to speak to write out what they plan to say. Suggest that they write no more than one page single-spaced, as this will take about five minutes to read.

We all have seen services hijacked with bad theology and emotional meltdowns. This is not the time for the speaker to say something that will make others angry or even more distraught. As the leader of this process and ultimately of the service, it is your job to avoid this if at all possible.

Again, do all you can to effectively prepare and lead the family through the "valley of the shadow."

Days before the service, it is good to have a plan of calling and checking in on the family. This does not need to be done by the pastor but can be done by a key volunteer who has been introduced into the circle or someone who will be involved with the aftercare.

As the pastor prepares for the funeral, design a service that has prayers, Scriptures, music, and a sermon that will bless the family. All the time, it is important to remind yourself that your goals are to care for the family, to celebrate the deceased, and to honor God. Also be aware that sometimes family members will want a copy of your sermon, so prepare accordingly.

A good bulletin will help you care for those in attendance. Because there will probably be people at the service who are unchurched, it is a good idea to print out the Scripture and any liturgy in the bulletin, so they can take it home for further reflection. A good bulletin also allows for extra details such as directions to the cemetery or an invitation to a meal afterward. There can also be poems or the obituary printed on the back. A good bulletin is a detail that assures the family and attendees that your church cares about the service, and, by extension, that you care for them.

You may find it helpful to create a "bulletin script" with the full text of the service. This type of script allows everyone who is participating to know what to expect and keeps everyone on task so that all the elements flow together. This is especially helpful if you have participants who are not on your regular worship team. Transitions to set up Scripture and songs are very important to note as well.

As you prepare the sermon, be aware that you are crafting a "life message" that not only helps people celebrate and laugh but gives purpose and meaning to the deceased person's life. I like to set the person's picture in front of me as I write to remind me to do everything to honor the deceased and to be helpful to the family. As you decide on stories, do your best to decide what life lessons can be gleaned. Use adjectives that will help people see the big picture. After the life-story, be sure to include the spiritual or faith story of the person.

Words of assurance and delving deeply into the "why" question should be well thought-out and scripted. Your purpose here is to help people connect the dots. Create an image of the place that God has created for their loved one (John 14). In the event of an untimely death, help people remember that God weeps with them and that God whose Son died at an early age surely knows their sorrow better than anyone (Romans 8).

If appropriate to the situation, address the fact that accidents happen and that no one is to blame. Lastly, in the case of suicide, serve up as much mercy and grace as you can, knowing that everyone is hurting. You may feel the need to go over how mental health issues or untreated depression can go undetected, emphasizing again that no one is to blame. Drive home the point that God has great mercy for those who have made this choice but that this is not the way any life should have to end. Perhaps there is something in your doctrine that you can quote to help support you.

If you need help in preparing a message for a particular or difficult situation, resources are available. For example, see *Funeral Services* by Cynthia Danals. It is also a good idea to have a relationship with the funeral home director, who can tell you what the funeral home offers and what their procedures are—for example, whether you are to ride with the family to the graveside or to drive your own car. Also, as part of the planning, the funeral director may have already collected an honorarium for your services from the family.

Whenever you have a congregation of unchurched teens and the deceased has either died by accident or suicide, you have an incredible opportunity to do what the church can do best: offer the assurance of eternal life and the opportunity to live life in ways that honor God and the deceased. As difficult as these situations might seem, be encouraged, as these might be some of the most important times that you will have as a person of faith to make a difference.

On the day of the service, arrive early so you can make sure the sanctuary is prepared for the family. In my early years at The Church of the Resurrection, I worked closely with Reverend Adam Hamilton, who has always been willing to do whatever it takes to get the church ready. I saw him do everything from shake out the front doormats to wiping down the sinks. If you are having the service in an unknown place, be sure that you know the layout of the chancel, family rooms, and so forth. Plus, you will want to greet the family as they enter.

If the family is having visitation before the service, do your best to prepare the family before the guests start to arrive. This may be the first time they've ever experienced something like this. As you prepare for the doors to open to the guests, you might have the family center themselves in front of the casket and encourage them with the idea that "everyone is coming to offer you love and support. However, we want to make sure that you have your needs taken care of. Here are water and tissues for you and chairs or stools if you need to sit. Please, let us know if you have any other needs." Then offer them a prayer of comfort and assurance for the healing that this time might offer. Always make sure that someone is there to care for the family—either yourself or a key volunteer.

Usually the mortuary will coordinate:

- Moving and placement of the casket or urn

- Plot or niche space

- Flowers

- Processional to cemetery

- Visitation time, which can be at the mortuary or your church

- Obituary in the local newspaper

- Guest book

Before the actual service begins, it is customary to stand with the family to allow them one last time to view the body before the casket is closed. Once the casket is closed, invite the family to center themselves in a comfortable space. This is a time to get them emotionally and mentally ready.

Your leadership in these pre-service moments is important. Give the family clear instructions about how you will lead them in and where they are to sit. Again emphasize your intentions: to celebrate the life of their loved one, to comfort them, and to worship God. Once they see your readiness, they will feel as if they are in good hands and will find the courage to move forward. Remember that whereas you have probably done funerals before and are familiar with what happens, this may not be the case for many of the family members; it may be completely new for many of them. And remember that their grief may paralyze them in a number of ways.

A well-planned funeral service should be between forty-five minutes to an hour. If it is any longer, the unchurched will be glad they *only* come to funerals, and that is not what you want. They will assume that you preach that way all the time. In any event, you will want to end on a high note! The deceased is with God today. "Let us hold onto each other and help the family as they live forward."

Do not be hesitant in your hope. Radiate your faith that even the unchurched will want to come back for more. It is hard to imagine a greater tool for growing your church than a well-thought-out funeral. Yet do not underestimate the importance of good follow-up.

Very recently, a young pastor called to ask about how to care for his community, as they had just suffered the death of a teenager one week and then the next week a four-year-old had been tragically killed. We talked about being clear with the congregation: maybe the pastor needed to do a two- or three-week sermon series based on the "Why" questions: Why did God let this happen? Why do bad things happen to good people? Why do we hurt so badly? What did we do to deserve this?

This pastor definitely needed to engage volunteers to help him continue visits to these families. The pastor's presence was important, but he needed to mentor and guide others in this care process too. We talked about helping others know the right things to say. Sometimes not saying anything is best—that is, just BE lovingly present with people. I learned this lesson from a father whose fourteen-year-old had suffered from depression and had committed suicide. The father said one particular friend didn't try to say anything but rather just hugged him and allowed him to cry. Sometimes saying less is better because no words can take away the pain.

I also encouraged this young pastor to offer a five- or six-week grief class. There are several excellent group guides available. Or you might choose to do a book study to help your congregation. You could choose *When Bad Things Happen to Good People* by Rabbi Harold Kushner or *The Will of God* by Leslie Weatherhead. These are classics that help people navigate life's most difficult questions.

Finally, I encouraged the pastor to put important dates on his calendar in order to call or send a card. Anniversaries such as birthdays and dates of death are especially important as they are sure to stir up memories and feelings. If you continue to call even years after the event, you will be a hero. Not that you are seeking to be one, but you will find that the family will be so glad that you still remember their loved one. Aftercare is so important! And you must plan how you are going to do this. Have others help you, or aftercare will fall between the cracks of everything else that happens in your ministry.

Caring for You

Finally, let's talk about caring for you.

Ministry is fulfilling and wonderful. It can give your life purpose. Yet it can also drain you if you are not careful.

At the beginning of this book, I confessed to you about how I had literally fallen on my face on Easter morning. That was a clue. You may absolutely love what you do, but you must love yourself also. Take time without guilt to do those things that are most renewing to you. Make plans for vacations, play dates, movies, gardening, exercise, or whatever it is that keeps you healthy emotionally, physically, and spiritually. Eating right and getting good counsel are essential.

A Final Word About Redemption

In closing, let me remind you that God has anointed you to do this holy work. What you do offers redemption and restoration to individuals, family systems, your community, and truly the whole world. God also anoints you to help others in your congregation find their calling, their ways to minister and care for others. Caring for the congregation is not a solo task; it is a way of living together as the body of Christ.

As we began this book together with a prayer, let me end in this way:

> *Gracious, holy God, thank you for the chance to lead your people through life's challenging valleys. Allow us to help others so your light might shine anew in their lives. We offer ourselves to you that you might guide our footsteps, our voices, and our every move to show people the way of your Son, Jesus the Christ. Amen.*

Questions and Reflections

Do you have key phrases that you incorporate into your funeral services?
Articulate your personal theology about death and resurrection.
How do you walk with the family when death is imminent?

- What is your standard to lead the family through the death process?

- How do you care for the family after death?

- Do you go immediately after the family calls?

How do you articulate the gospel message of hope to the non- and nominally religious?

Is your funeral service prepared with the purpose of

- honoring the deceased?

- comforting the family?

- inviting the non- and nominally religious to receive the gospel message of resurrection and hope?

What is your plan for follow-up for the first month? first year? subsequent years?

Can you give an example of when you saw redemption happening in the midst of a family's journey through "the valley of the shadow of death"?

What events helped that redemption happen?

Anointing

In the United Methodist tradition, anointing with oil offers an opportunity for spiritual healing affirmed by Scripture in James 5:13-15. This prayer of faith says, "Is any one of you in trouble? He should pray. Is anyone happy? Let him sing songs of praise. Is any one of you sick? He should call the elders of the church to pray over him and anoint him with oil in the name of the Lord. And the prayer offered in faith will make the sick person well; the Lord will raise him up" (NIV).

The United Methodist Book of Worship notes that "anointing the forehead with oil is a sign act invoking the healing love of God. The oil points beyond itself and those doing the anointing to the action of the Holy Spirit and the presence of the healing Christ, who is God's Anointed One."*

Anointing gives the opportunity for spiritual healing, which is a wholeness of body, mind, and spirit. The oil reminds us of God's promise of presence with those who are sick or suffering. Anointing offers *healing* and not *curing*, being made whole in the love of Christ.

Anointing people who are frail is a powerful reminder of God's triune presence in their journey, offering the peace that they do

---

* *The United Methodist Book of Worship* (Nashville: The United Methodist Publishing House, 1992), 614.

not travel alone and helping complete their *Circle of Faith* at the end of life.

When anointing someone who is frail:

Explain anointing and get the person's permission (or the permission of family present).

The frail person may not be familiar with anointing in the United Methodist tradition. Explain what it is and how you will do it. Ask them if this is something they would like to experience.

Read the passage from James 5:13-15.

After reading the Scripture passage, remind the person that this anointing is not offered as a *cure*, but instead as inviting the Holy Spirit to be present with them, offering wholeness in the love of Christ.

Anoint with oil in the name of the Father, Son, and Holy Spirit.

With anointing oil on the thumb, make the sign of the cross on the person's forehead, saying, "I anoint you with oil in the name of the Father, Son, and Holy Spirit."

Pray the Lord's Prayer.

Pray the Lord's Prayer together.

Read Psalm 23.

Conclude by reading Psalm 23, reminding the person that God walks with us *through* our valleys, our dark times.

Some Scripture Passages to Use in Congregational Care

Ephesians 3:20-21 NIV

Now to him who is able to do immeasurably more than all we ask or imagine, according to his power that is at work within us, to him be glory in the church and in Christ Jesus throughout all generations, for ever and ever! Amen.

Romans 12:12 NIV

Be joyful in hope, patient in affliction, faithful in prayer.

Psalm 145:18 NIV

The LORD is near to all who call on him,
    to all who call on him in truth.

Colossians 4:2 NIV

Devote yourselves to prayer, being watchful and thankful.

1 John 5:14-15 NIV

This is the confidence we have in approaching God: that if we ask anything according to his will, he hears us. And if we know that he hears us—whatever we ask—we know that we have what we asked of him.

1 Thessalonians 5:16-18 NIV

Be joyful always; pray continually; give thanks in all circumstances, for this is God's will for you in Christ Jesus.

Psalm 19:14 NIV

May the words of my mouth and the meditation of my heart
be pleasing in your sight,
O LORD, my Rock and my Redeemer.

Romans 8:26-27 NIV

In the same way, the Spirit helps us in our weakness. We do not know what we ought to pray for, but the Spirit himself intercedes for us with groans that words cannot express. And he who searches our hearts knows the mind of the Spirit, because the Spirit intercedes for the saints in accordance with God's will.

Philippians 4:6-7 NIV

Do not be anxious about anything, but in everything, by prayer and petition, with thanksgiving, present your requests to God. And the peace of God, which transcends all understanding, will guard your hearts and your minds in Christ Jesus.

Psalm 106:1 NIV

Praise the LORD.
Give thanks to the LORD, for he is good;
his love endures forever.

James 1:5-6 NIV

If any of you lacks wisdom, he should ask God, who gives generously to all without finding fault, and it will be given to him. But when he asks, he must believe and not doubt, because he who doubts is like a wave of the sea, blown and tossed by the wind.

1 Peter 5:6-10

Humble yourselves therefore under the mighty hand of God, so that he may exalt you in due time. Cast all your anxiety on him, because he cares for you. Discipline yourselves, keep alert. Like a roaring lion your adversary the devil prowls around, looking for someone to devour. Resist him, steadfast in your faith, for you know that your brothers and sisters in all the world are undergoing the same kinds of suffering. And after you have suffered for a little while, the God of all grace, who has called you to his eternal glory in Christ, will himself restore, support, strengthen, and establish you.

Psalm 34:4 NIV

I sought the LORD, and he answered me;
  he delivered me from all my fears.

Proverbs 3:5-6 NIV

Trust in the LORD with all your heart
  and lean not on your own understanding;
in all your ways acknowledge him,
  and he will make your paths straight.

Hebrews 12:14-15

Pursue peace with everyone, and the holiness without which no one will see the Lord. See to it that no one fails to obtain the grace of God; that no root of bitterness springs up and causes trouble, and through it many become defiled.

Isaiah 43:1-5

But now thus says the LORD,
  he who created you, O Jacob,
  he who formed you, O Israel:

Do not fear, for I have redeemed you;

> I have called you by name, you are mine.

When you pass through the waters, I will be with you;

> and through the rivers, they shall not overwhelm you;

when you walk through fire you shall not be burned,

> and the flame shall not consume you.

For I am the LORD your God,

> the Holy One of Israel, your Savior.

I give Egypt as your ransom,

> Ethiopia and Seba in exchange for you.

Because you are precious in my sight,

> and honored, and I love you,

I give people in return for you,

> nations in exchange for your life.

Do not fear, for I am with you;

> I will bring your offspring from the east,
>
> and from the west I will gather you.

John 14:1-6 NIV
Grief and Loss

"Do not let your hearts be troubled. Trust in God; trust also in me. In my Father's house are many rooms; if it were not so, I would have told you. I am going there to prepare a place for you. And if I go and prepare a place for you, I will come back and take you to be with me that you also may be where I am. You know the way to the place where I am going."

Thomas said to him, "Lord, we don't know where you are going, so how can we know the way?"

Jesus answered, "I am the way and the truth and the life. No one comes to the Father except through me."

Psalm 23

The LORD is my shepherd, I shall not want.
   He makes me lie down in green pastures;
he leads me beside still waters;
   he restores my soul.
He leads me in right paths
   for his name's sake.

Even though I walk through the darkest valley,
   I fear no evil;
for you are with me;
   your rod and your staff—
   they comfort me.

You prepare a table before me
   in the presence of my enemies;
you anoint my head with oil;
   my cup overflows.
Surely goodness and mercy shall follow me
   all the days of my life,
and I shall dwell in the house of the LORD
   my whole life long.

Romans 8:35, 37-39 NIV

Who shall separate us from the love of Christ? Shall trouble or hardship or persecution or famine or nakedness or danger or sword? . . . No, in all these things we are more than conquerors through him who loved us. For I am convinced that neither death nor life, neither angels nor demons, neither the present nor the future, nor any powers, neither height nor depth, nor anything else in all creation, will be able to separate us from the love of God that is in Christ Jesus our Lord.

2 Corinthians 5:1, 4-8 NIV

Now we know that if the earthly tent we live in is destroyed, we have a building from God, an eternal house in heaven, not built by human hands. . . . For while we are in this tent, we groan and are burdened, because we do not wish to be unclothed but to be clothed with our heavenly dwelling, so that what is mortal may be swallowed up by life. Now it is God who has made us for this very purpose and has given us the Spirit as a deposit, guaranteeing what is to come.

Therefore we are always confident and know that as long as we are at home in the body we are away from the Lord. We live by faith, not by sight. We are confident, I say, and would prefer to be away from the body and at home with the Lord.

Revelation 21:1-5

Then I saw a new heaven and a new earth; for the first heaven and the first earth had passed away, and the sea was no more. And I saw the holy city, the new Jerusalem, coming down out of heaven from God, prepared as a bride adorned for her husband. And I heard a loud voice from the throne saying,

"See, the home of God is among mortals.
He will dwell with them;
they will be his peoples,
and God himself will be with them;
he will wipe every tear from their eyes.
Death will be no more;
mourning and crying and pain will be no more,
for the first things have passed away."

And the one who was seated on the throne said, "See, I am making all things new."

APPENDIX C

Congregational Care Minister (CCM) Description

Congregational Care Ministers

A Program for Volunteer Lay Ministry

A focus in congregational care will be to develop a ministry where the pastor will have a team of five to twelve lay-persons, called Congregational Care Ministers (CCMs), to meet the care needs of our church family.

Congregational Care Ministers will meet regularly as a team with the pastor for supervision and assignments. They can make hospital calls, telephone persons in need of contact, meet one-on-one with persons needing a listening ear for prayer and encouragement, offer support to grieving families, and proactively seek to encourage and care for persons within their pastorate. This partnership between lay and clergy will enable us to provide another level of care.

Congregational Care Ministers

Requirements and Application

Requirements for Serving as a Congregational Care Minister

Because Congregational Care Ministers will be offering some of the care previously done only by the pastor, it is important that these persons have basic theological and biblical training. It is recommended that Congregational Care Ministers complete at least **one year** of Disciple Bible Study plus another intensive Bible course such as:

- The Alpha Course

- Christian Believer

- Companions in Christ

- Stephen Ministries training

Congregational Care Ministers will also be required to be certified through The United Methodist Church's *Safe and Sacred Spaces* training.

Required Training for Congregational Care Ministers

Congregational Care Ministers will be required to complete the *Congregational Care Ministers Training Course*. This six-week course covers information on Sacred Spaces, Methodism, Hospital Visits, Boundaries, Counseling, Prayer, Funeral, and Older Adult Ministries.

Other Requirements

Congregational Care Ministers must have been active members of the church for at least **three years**. They must be fulfilling the four expectations of our members: attending worship each weekend except when sick or out of town, actively pursuing growth in the Christian life through participation in a small group or in some other form of Christian discipleship, serving God with their time in the ministry of the church, and giving financially in proportion to their income with the tithe being the goal.

Congregational Care Ministers will be required to agree to and sign the Volunteer Leader Covenant.

Congregational Care Ministers will be expected to commit three hours per week to this ministry.

Please respond to the following questions:

1. Why do you want to be a Congregational Care Minister?

2. What does it mean to be a deeply committed Christian (or perhaps disciple)?

3. Do you practice any spiritual disciplines? If so, what are they?

4. Write a one-page spiritual (or faith) autobiography.

Volunteer Leader Covenant

Our lay leaders, along with our staff, fulfill the biblical roles of elders and deacons, shepherds and teachers. Throughout the New Testament, leaders are called to be examples to the rest of the church. As leaders, they are held to higher standards than other members. Paul sets forth lists of attributes of elders and deacons in his letters to the early church. Leaders should be "above reproach" and "not be puffed up with conceit," among other things. Peter, likewise, challenges leaders to be "examples to the flock" and to exercise leadership with a willing heart. Because leaders are held to a higher standard, James says, "not many of you should become teachers, because you know that we who teach will be judged more strictly."

As leaders, we set the tone and pace for the entire congregation. We model the Christian faith, the Christian life, and the attitude and heart of a Christian for our congregation. We shape the heart, character, and life of this Christian community. For this reason, it is vital that we walk the Christian walk. Spiritually healthy leaders will produce a spiritually healthy church. Likewise, leaders who fail to walk with Christ will have devastating consequences.

With this in mind, the following covenant was developed to guide our life together as leaders. We use these standards to hold ourselves accountable to pursuing the Christian life. And in so doing, we recognize that it is God's grace that calls forth our faithful response, and it is God's grace that brings such transformation in our lives.

I. The Goal of the Christian Life: Sanctification

Jesus summarized the goal of the Christian life with two commandments: love the Lord our God with all your heart, soul, mind, and strength; and love your neighbor as yourself. John Wesley spoke of this goal as *sanctification, Christian perfection,* or *holiness.* In our Methodist tradition, three *General Rules* were designed to help Christians pursue this goal. As leaders we pursue these "rules" as we grow in faith and service together.

A. Avoid those things that are inconsistent with the life of faith, separate us from God, and bring harm to others, such as:

1. Self-destructive behavior (addictive behavior, poor self-care)
2. Moral compromise (sexual misconduct, greed, dishonesty)
3. Self-centeredness and pride
4. Malice (harboring resentment, acting in anger, backbiting)
5. Wasting of resources (the church's, or personal resources of time, talent, finance)

B. Do good of every possible sort, such as:

1. Live a life of love
2. Share our faith inside and outside of Resurrection

3. Care for our families

4. Build others up

5. Be engaged with those in need, both inside the church and out

C. Pursue growth in our spiritual lives, such as:

1. Attend worship each weekend, except when sick or out of town

2. Engage in close Christian friendships for spiritual growth and accountability in a small group

3. Serve God with our time and talents

4. Give in proportion to our income, with the tithe being the goal

5. Spend time in prayer and in the personal study of Scripture

II. The Heart and Attitude of a Leader

A. What is the heart and attitude of a leader?

1. Humble (servanthood)

2. Positive

3. Joyful

4. Committed to Christ

5. Devoted to the purpose and vision of the church

B. How will our leaders live toward one another?

1. Demonstrating respect and grace

2. Accepting differences

3. Maintaining appropriate confidentiality

4. Publicly supporting other volunteer leaders, pastors, and staff members

5. Going directly to the individual whenever a problem arises

III. The Faith and Character of a United Methodist

(edit as necessary to fit your denominational credo)

We are a United Methodist Church. We expect our leaders to honor our denominational heritage and to pursue ministry in keeping with our tradition.

United Methodists are people who seek to love and serve God with our head, our heart, and our hands. We are orthodox in faith, liberal in spirit, passionate and deeply devoted to Christ, and desire to be wholly surrendered to God. We bring together both the evangelical and social gospel—inviting people to a life-transforming relationship with Jesus Christ, and then equipping and challenging them to live their faith in the public sphere, being engaged in the issues of our time and seeking to shape a world that looks more like the kingdom of God. Methodists have been known as "reasonable enthusiasts"—valuing both a personal, passionate faith and one that is intellectually informed. Methodists are constantly looking to connect our faith to the world in meaningful, relevant ways. Methodists value spiritual disciplines and a "methodical" approach to growing in the faith. We strive for both personal holiness and social holiness.

United Methodists are not afraid to ask difficult questions, to take on tough subjects, and to admit that we do not always understand the answers. We are "people of the Book"—holding the Bible to be the inspired Word from God and encouraging people to read, study, and live by its words. "While we acknowledge the primacy of Scripture in theological reflection, our attempts to grasp its meaning always involve experience, tradition and reason. Like Scripture, these become creative vehicles of the Holy Spirit as they function within the church."* Methodists also believe the Bible came to us through people who heard God's Word in the light of their own cultural and historical circumstances. And hence, we study the Scriptures carefully, making use of scholarship and asking critical questions. And, as Methodists encounter theological differences among Christians, we bear in mind John Wesley's approach, "in essentials, unity; in nonessentials, liberty; in all things, charity."†

Methodists are people who love God with all our heart, soul, mind, and strength, and love our neighbors. We pursue acts of piety toward God and acts of mercy toward others. We value passionate worship, relevant preaching, small groups to hold Christians accountable to one another, the need to address the social issues of our time, and the need to be people whose faith is firmly rooted in and built upon the Scriptures. Methodists value the full participation of women and men, people of all races, classes, and backgrounds, in all facets of fellowship and leadership within the church and society.

This is our heritage, and it continues to shape (*church name*) in every area of our ministry.

Covenant

I have read the above and am committed to living my life and pursuing ministry in a way that is consistent with these expectations, and desire to do so at (*church name*).

Name _____ Date _____

---

* From *The Book of Discipline of the United Methodist Church 2004* (Nashville: The United Methodist Publishing House, 2004) ¶ 104.

† *Book of Discipline*, ¶ 102. Revised June 2005.

Counseling Intake Paperwork

Congregational Care

Authorization for Referral and Team Case Management

Congregational care is guided by a team of counselors, pastors, care coordinators, a spiritual director, and a clinical psychologist to meet the spiritual, emotional, physical, and relational needs in our lives. At times, it is necessary to share background from your client file to effectively assess, direct, and carry out this holistic care. Likewise, multiple members of our team may interact with the client and collaborate in the caring process.

By signing this form, I give the undersigned pastor(s) permission to present my case and details of my client file with the staff members of the church when necessary for the advancement of my care. If a pastor does refer me to a resource in the community, this authorization also allows that resource person to follow up with me via e-mail or phone within 60 days to receive feedback regarding that referral. I understand that these decisions will be made in an ethical and responsible manner.

In order to honor your time and the pastor's time, each counseling appointment will be limited to one hour.

_____

Client Signature   **Date**

_____

Pastor Signature   **Date**

Pastoral Care Notes

Member Name: _____

Date: _____, 20_____   Phone _____ In Person _____

Person(s) Present:

Personal History:

Concerns:

Biblical Passages/Other Care Offered:

Danger Signs: suicide, abuse, etc.   No_____ Yes_____

Referrals:

Safety and Self-Care Contract

I, _____, commit
to work toward my own health and safety and the health and safety
of others. If I feel as though I might harm myself or someone else,
I agree to follow the action steps listed below and ask for help.

I will call one or more of the following people to discuss my feelings:

_____

_____

_____

I will do one or more of the following things to help me manage
difficult feelings:

_____

_____

_____

I will seek additional support in one or more of the following ways:

_____

_____

_____

Today I met with _____,
a staff member at *(name of church)*. My signature below indicates
that I am refusing emergency assistance and am well enough to
leave the church of my own accord.

Emergency 911
Pastor Emergency Pager ....
Suicide Crisis Line ....
National Suicide Prevention Helpline 1-800-273-8255
Local Psychiatric Center Crisis Line ....
Domestic Violence Hotline ....

Signature_____ Date_____

Congregational Care Counseling Guide

In providing counseling, it is first and foremost important to listen. As you listen, the Spirit may help you direct the conversation. As pastors and caregivers, it is important to provide spiritual care. In each conversation, open in prayer, and begin the time with opening questions such as: "What brings you here today? What is going on lately? How can the church be of help?" After listening to the answers and engaging in conversation, a few topics may arise. Choose the most predominant topic. Some topics are listed below with signs to look for, talking points, Scriptures, suggested reading, and resources. There are some topics and conversations that indicate the need for a person to see a licensed counselor. Do not hesitate to refer. At the end of the conversation, always suggest coming to worship weekly and using some type of daily devotion or Bible study.

Anger

Talking Points/Facts

- Anger is a trailhead that points to some hurt in your life.

- To find healing for that anger:

  Step 1. When you get angry, ask, "Why does *this* of all things make me so angry?"

  Step 2. Follow that question until you find the wound that you tend to lock up.

  Step 3. Ask Jesus in prayer to heal that pain that is employing anger to help it.

  Step 4. Schedule an appointment with a pastor and maybe a therapist to talk about it.

  Step 5. The goal is not to erase the hurt, but to recognize it and find better ways of finding healing for it than getting angry.

- Counting to ten or giving space to oneself can be helpful when enraged.

Scriptures

James 1:19
Mark 1:40-42
Ephesians 4:29-32
Hebrews 12:14-15

Prayer

> *Savior Jesus, my anger has not provided the healing, respect, and intimacy that I want. Forgive me for the ways that I have*

hurt others. I place the hurt that is causing my anger in your hands. Heal me, Lord Jesus. I need you. Amen.

Suggested Reading

Anger by Gary Chapman. Chicago: Northfield, 2007.
The Angry Book by Theodore I. Rubin. New York: Touchstone, 1997.
The Art of Forgiving by Lewis B. Smedes. New York: Ballantine, 1996.
The Dance of Anger by Harriet Lerner. New York: HarperCollins, 1997.
Forgive and Forget: Healing the Hurts We Don't Deserve by Lewis Smedes. New York: HarperOne, 2007.
You Are the One You've Been Waiting For by Richard C. Schwartz. Oak Park, Ill.: Center for Self Leadership, 2008.

Resources

Anger management classes

Anxiety

Talking Points

- Listen to the anxiety—what wisdom and instruction is it imparting to me?

- Some degree of anxiety can be good.

- Fear differs from anxiety.

- Legitimate fears have an object, but obsessive worry can cause unhealthy anxiety.

- In the Bible, the Greek word for *anxiety* comes from two root words meaning "divide" and "mind."

- Believe you are a child of God and that you are loved.

- Ask yourself, what is the root cause?

- Can you name your triggers, the things that cause you anxiety?

- Why would you stay stuck in anxiety patterns?

- What is to be gained by giving up anxiety?

- What would you do for God if you had no anxiety?

- Name one thing that is overwhelming. What is the most important?

Scriptures

Philippians 4:4-7 Peace surpassing understanding

Romans 8:38-39 Nothing separates us from the love of God

Matthew 6:25-34 Do not worry

Genesis 1:31 God creates humans good, before we do anything to deserve our worth

Isaiah 43:1-5 Do not fear, for I have redeemed you; I have called you by name, you are mine. When you pass through the waters, I will be with you; and through the rivers, they shall not overwhelm you.

1 Peter 5:7-11 Cast all your anxiety on him, because he cares for you.

Ephesians 3:20 He's able to accomplish abundantly far more than all we can ask or imagine

1 John 4:16b-21 There is no fear in love, but perfect love casts out fear

Proverbs 3:5-6 Trust in the Lord and not on your own understanding

Prayer

- Breath prayer: Repeat one phrase such as "Be near me, Lord Jesus." Take two to three deep breaths. Repeat for two minutes.

- The Serenity Prayer

Suggested Reading

Anxiety Attacked: Applying Scripture to the Cares of the Soul by John MacArthur Jr. Colorado Springs: Cook Communications Ministries, 1993.
The Breath of Life: A Simple Way to Pray by Ron DelBene. Nashville: Upper Room Books, 1996.
Embracing the Fear: Learning to Manage Anxiety & Panic Attacks by Judith Bemis and Amr Barrada. Center City, Minn.: Hazelden, 1994.
Fearless Relationships: Simple Rules for Lifelong Contentment by Karen Casey. Center City, Minn.: Hazelden, 2003.
Paths to Prayer: Finding Your Own Way to the Presence of God by Patricia D. Brown. San Francisco: Jossey-Bass, 2003.
You Are the One You've Been Waiting For by Richard C. Schwartz. Oak Park, Ill.: Center for Self Leadership, 2008.

Resources

Celebrate Recovery
National Anxiety Foundation (859) 281-0003
Kansas City Center for Anxiety Treatment (913) 649-8820
www.coping.com
www.overcomepanic.com
Pastoral counseling
Community-based counseling
Serenity Prayer

Cancer or Chronic Illness

Talking Points

- Love the physical part of me that carries the cancer or other chronic illness. Take care of it.

- Focus on the treatment opportunities.

- Find joy in the adversity when possible.

• For supporters, be with them where they are—
whether in pain or as cheerleaders.

Scriptures

James 5:13-15

Psalm 121

Isaiah 43:1-7

Lamentations 3:32

Psalm 63:8

2 Corinthians 4:8

Hebrews 12:2

Philippians 4:13

1 Peter 5:7

Prayer

> *Lord, you said that when we walk through the water, you will be with us; we are precious in your sight and you love us. In this time of health trial and adversity, I need your presence more than ever. Lord, some days I feel hard-pressed on every side, but with you at my side I do not feel crushed. Struck down at times, but not destroyed. This disease makes me feel as if I don't have any control. Lord, give me strength and courage, hold me in the palm of your hand, and give me peace.*

Suggested Reading

Jesus Calling by Sarah Young. Nashville: Thomas Nelson, 2004.

Jesus Lives by Sarah Young. Nashville: Thomas Nelson, 2009.

What About Divine Healing? A Study of Christian Healing by Susan Sonnenday Vogel. Nashville: Abingdon Press, 2004.

The Will of God by Leslie Weatherhead. Nashville: Abingdon Press, 1999.

Resources

Cancer support groups

Ongoing pastoral care and counseling opportunities from the church

American Cancer Society

Caring Conversations, www.practicalbioethics.org.

Depression

Talking Points

- Listen to understand the message of the depression. It's trying to tell you something.

- It is very important to break the cycle of the negative rumination that is part of depression.

- What is good about me?

- Who is your support system?

- Helpful tools to combat depression include: exercise, omega-3s, sunshine, social activity, sleep, and diet.

Scriptures
Jeremiah 29:11
Proverbs 2:3-5
Psalm 13:1-3
Psalm 34:18
Psalm 56
Philippians 4:13-14
Job 19:7-10
Luke 1:13
Isaiah 43:1-2, 5, 18-19

Sermons

Depression by Karen Lampe, May 2005. Available at www.cor.org.

Suggested Reading

The Depression Cure by Stephen S. Ilardi. Cambridge, Mass.: Da Capo, 2009.

Finding Hope Again: Overcoming Depression by Neil T. Anderson and Baumchen. Ventura, Calif.: Regal, 2000.

The Freedom from Depression Workbook by Les Carter and Frank Minirth. Nashville: Thomas Nelson, 1995.

Reaching for the Invisible God by Philip Yancey. Grand Rapids: Zondervan, 2000.

Prayer

> *Healing God, we celebrate your power to bring light to the darkness and healing and comfort to those in need. Your ways are mysterious and wonderful and too vast for us to comprehend. As the Great Physician, be with us through moments of despair and hopelessness. Grant us hope and assurance that our lives will be surrounded by your love and comfort. May we find the tools that will help in this difficult journey. In Christ's name. Amen.*

Resources

Counselor

www.Godtest.org, Mental Health Questions

Celebrate Recovery, www.celebraterecovery.com

Depression support groups

The Burns Depression Checklist, www.suicideforum.com/bdc/index.html.

Grief

Talking Points

- Grief includes a sadness that is unique to and a natural response toward loss.

- Plan ways to grieve.

- Talk out loud with a trusted confidant (or journal) about the feelings you're experiencing. And in naming/being honest about all your feelings (which may be conflicting and seem irrational to you), recognize that there is nothing wrong with your feelings (and nothing wrong with you because you have those feelings). Working through how you will choose to respond to those feelings is important (and this is the critical work that you will have to do in order to heal), but recognize that there is nothing "wrong" with any varied feelings that you might experience.

- When you ask the "why" question (and you will), recognize that while there may be rationally descriptive answers to that question (for example, *my loved one died because [he/she] was riding on the passenger's side going northbound when a westbound driver ran the stoplight . . .* Or, *my loved one died because [he/she] had cancer cells in [his/her] body that took away the ability of vital organs to function*). Those answers—while true and accurate—likely won't alleviate the nagging question of "Yes, but why my loved one?" You must recognize that this is very normal. And when you are especially occupied with *Why me?/Why my loved one?* (which is very natural for most people), try asking out loud the opposite question that is, "*Why not me? These are the kinds of things that people experience every day in this fallen world, so why do I think that I should be exempt?*" When you ask yourself (and God) this question, you might be surprised (and perhaps helped) by what the honest answers to that question are.

- Above all, remember that through the unconditional love of Jesus Christ we are Easter people: we are people of the Resurrection. This means that above all,

you must recognize that your grief is for *your* loss—
not your loved one's. You will certainly grieve that
you no longer have your loved one close to you, and
you may certainly grieve for what you perceive your
loved one suffered prior to death, but upon going
through death, your loved one is in the shepherding
arms and eternal care of God (see Romans 8:35, 37-
39). And the same shepherding arms and eternal care
of God that your loved one now fully experiences—
well, this is yours as well!

Scriptures

Psalm 23
Isaiah 43:1-3
Romans 8
1 Corinthians 15
John 14:1-7
Revelation 21

Sermons (by Adam Hamilton)

Where Was God When . . .—This three-part series was preached
in January 2001.
The Bible and the Afterlife—This four-part series was preached in
April 2005.
God's Will for Your Life—Preached August 2010.
    All sermons are accessible at www.cor.org.

Prayer

> *Lord, be to me what you promise in Psalm 23. I need your
> grace and strength in order to want to move forward; I need
> the faith to believe you and I need the ability that you alone
> can give to release my loved one to your eternal care. Lord,
> help me be honest about my feelings and keep me from the
> tendency to choose bitterness and resentment. Give me the*

grace to take one day at a time and to commit each feeling and memory to your eternal care. Help me celebrate and live into the good memories without those causing me pain. Help me choose forgiveness wherever it's needed. Above all, own me with the promise of the Resurrection and salvation's gift of one day seeing my loved one again . . . eternally.

Suggested Reading

Grief Books from Stephen Ministry
And Then Mark Died: Letters of Grief, Love, and Faith by Susan Sonnenday Vogel. Nashville: Abingdon Press, 2003.
Disappointment with God by Philip Yancey. Grand Rapids: Zondervan, 1988.
Finding Your Way after the Suicide of Someone You Love, by David B. Biebel & Suzanne L. Foster. Grand Rapids: Zondervan, 2005.
Good Grief by Granger E. Westberg. Minneapolis: Augsburg Fortress, 1997.
The Holy Longing by Ronald Rolheiser. New York, Doubleday, 1999. See, especially, the chapter titled "A Spirituality of the Paschal Mystery."
Lament for a Son by Nicholas Wolterstorff. Grand Rapids: Eerdmans, 1987.
Life After the Death of My Son by Dennis L. Apple. Kansas City: Beacon Hill, 2008.
The Shack by William P. Young. Newbury Park, Calif.: Windblown, 2007.
When Grief Breaks Your Heart by James W. Moore. Nashville: Abingdon Press, 1995.
The Will of God by Leslie Weatherhead. Nashville: Abingdon Press, 1972.

For Children

The Fall of Freddie the Leaf by Leo F. Buscaglia. Thorofare, N.J.: SLACK, 1982.
Tear Soup by Pat Schweibert and Chuck DeKlyen. Portland, Ore.: Grief Watch, 2005.

Water Bugs & Dragonflies: Explaining Death to Young Children by Doris
Stickney. Cleveland: Pilgrim, 1997.
What's Heaven? By Maria Shriver. New York: St. Martin's, 2007.

Resources

GriefShare, www.griefshare.org
Grief groups

Divorce

Talking Points

- Your worth is not tied to your marital status. At your
  creation, God called you "very good."

- Divorce is a painful split. Dating immediately following a divorce can stifle the healing you need as you
  try to find healing in another person.

- You will need to eventually forgive, for your sake.
  Forgiveness blesses you as you release the control the
  ex-spouse has over your feelings.

- Forgiving too soon can be hazardous to your healing.
  When you do forgive, forgive with your own ritual,
  for example, writing forgiveness on paper and burning
  it. Saying "I forgive you" to an ex-spouse often incites
  more anger and pain.

- Parents: During a divorce,

  1. Do not parentify your kids of all ages, treating
  them as your caregiver (parent) or as your best buddy
  instead of as your kids.
  2. Make space for your kids of all ages to share their
  pain even if their pain causes you hurt or guilt. They
  need you.

3. Pay attention to teenage girls who are more likely than boys to behave in overly sexualized ways or to begin an eating disorder or cutting.

Scriptures

Philippians 3:12-15

Genesis 1:31—Your worth is not tied to your marital status. At your creation, God called you "very good."

Prayer

> *God of infinite love and understanding, pour out your healing Spirit upon* _____ *as he or she reflects upon the failure of his or her marriage and makes a new beginning. Where there is hurt or bitterness, grant healing of memories and the ability to put behind the things that are past. Where feelings of despair or worthlessness flood in, nurture the spirit of hope and confidence that by your grace tomorrow can be better than yesterday. Heal their children and help us minister your healing to them. We pray for other family and friends, for the healing of their hurts and the acceptance of new realities. All this we ask in the name of the One who sets us free from slavery to the past and makes all things new, even Jesus Christ our Savior. Amen.*

Suggested Reading

Radical Recovery: Transforming the Despair of Your Divorce into an Unexpected Good by Suzy Brown. Abilene, Tex.: Leafwood, 2007.

Resources

Divorce recovery groups
Marriage and family therapists
List of the effects of divorce on children

Recommended Resources

The following list includes recommended reading from the Congregational Care staff and volunteers at The Church of the Resurrection.

Allen, Ronald J. *Hearing the Sermon: Relationship, Content, Feeling.* St. Louis: Chalice, 2004.

Bounds, Edward M. *The Complete Works of E. M. Bounds on Prayer: Experience the Wonders of God Through Prayer.* Grand Rapids: Baker Books, 2004.

Bridges, William. *Transitions: Making Sense of Life's Changes.* New York: Perseus Books, 1980.

Cloud, Henry, and John Townsend. *Boundaries: When to Say Yes, When to Say No, To Take Control of Your Life.* Grand Rapids: Zondervan, 1992.

Doka, Kenneth J., and Amy S. Tucci. *Living with Grief: Children and Adolescents.* Oregon, Ill.: Quality Books, 2008.

Evans, Abigail Rian. *Healing Liturgies for the Seasons of Life.* Louisville: Westminster John Knox, 2004.

Gerkin, Charles V. *An Introduction to Pastoral Care.* Nashville: Abingdon Press, 1997.

Guntzelman, Joan. *124 Prayers for Caregivers.* Liguori, Mo.: Liguori, 2002.

Kornfeld, Margaret Zipse. *Cultivating Wholeness: A Guide to Care and Counseling in Faith Communities.* New York: Continuum, 2000.

Kushner, Harold S. *When Bad Things Happen to Good People.* New York: Anchor, 2004.

Lebacqz, Karen. *Ethics and Spiritual Care: A Guide for Pastors and Spiritual Directors.* Nashville: Abingdon Press, 2000.

Maxwell, Katie. *Bedside Manners: A Practical Guide to Visiting the Ill.* Grand Rapids: Baker Books, 2005.

Mitchell, Kenneth R., and Herbert Anderson. *All Our Losses, All Our Griefs.* Louisville: Westminster John Knox, 1983.

Palenschus, Henry. *Personal Prayers in Times of Illness: A Personal Prayer Book.* Nashville: Abingdon Press, 2002.

Patton, John. *Pastoral Care: An Essential Guide.* Nashville: Abingdon Press, 2005.

Phillips, Sara Webb. *Pastoral Prayers for the Hospital Visit.* Nashville: Abingdon Press, 2006.

Shannon, Thomas A., and Charles N. Faso. *Let Them Go Free: A Guide to Withdrawing Life Support.* Washington, D.C.: Georgetown University Press, 2007.

Stevenson-Moessner, Jeanne. *A Primer in Pastoral Care.* Minneapolis: Augsburg Fortress, 2005.

Stone, Douglas, Bruce Patton, and Sheila Heen. *Difficult Conversations: How to Discuss What Matters Most.* New York: Penguin, 2000.

Switzer, David K. *Pastoral Care Emergencies.* Minneapolis: Augsburg Fortress, 2000.

United Methodist Publishing House. *The United Methodist Book of Worship (Pastor's Pocket Edition).* Nashville: The United Methodist Publishing House, 1994.

Vogel, Linda J. *Rituals for Resurrection: Celebrating Life and Death.* Nashville: Upper Room Books, 1996.

Vogel, Susan Sonnenday. *And Then Mark Died: Letters of Grief, Love, and Faith.* Nashville: Abingdon Press, 2003.

———. *Faith Questions: What About Divine Healing? A Study of Christian Healing.* Nashville: Abingdon Press, 2004.

Wolterstorff, Nicholas. *Lament for a Son.* Grand Rapids: Eerdmans, 1987.